Defeated

By James Voytek

Published by Pen It! Publications, LLC

812-371-4128 www.penitpublications.com

ISBN: 978-1-952894-39-8

Cover Design by Donna Cook

Edited by Sheila Shontz

Contents

Introduction

Like many people during high school, I had no idea what I wanted to do with my life. I had the boyhood dream many kids have to be a professional athlete, but the good lord did not bless me with the physical tools and I quickly realized that wasn't going to happen. I then wanted to be a sports broadcaster, commentating on sporting events and capturing those moments for the viewers at home. That field seemed ultra-competitive and nearly impossible to get started, and even harder to make a living at it.

I eventually landed on teaching. I am always honest with my students when I tell them I was not a great student. I did what I needed to get by, handing in assignments with halfhearted effort, scraping by with a C's in most classes, and in math mostly D's. The one class I almost always excelled in was English. I loved to write stories and journals about my life and experiences. I was by no means the next Shakespeare but got compliments from my high school teachers that they would save my pieces for the end to have something to look forward to. Those comments stuck with me and motivated me to write more and look into a career as an English teacher. It has not been a seamless road, in fact, I looked into other careers after student teaching, realizing how tough and demanding teaching can be. Some might have the perception that teachers have it made. They get out around two or three in the afternoon and have summers and weekends off. Many fail to account for the hours spent planning lessons, grading papers, contacting families, organizing activities, and attending professional development and other staff meetings. Not to mention trying to control twenty-five kids, and get them to pay attention and work hard. That in itself was enough to get me to rethink my career path.

I tried a year behind a desk answering phone calls for an IT company, and I realized how much I missed teaching. I missed conversations with my students, creating lessons that engage students and have them look at the world in a different perspective. I quickly applied to various schools in the Connecticut area and was lucky enough to get hired at a middle school in New Haven, Connecticut, where I have been ever since.

I have always had a love with writing. In college, I created some short stories about various topics where I got some of my best advice about writing. Professor Troy was my creative writing teacher and she impacted my life in ways she will never know. She gave specific feedback on my writing, pages upon pages of specific suggestions that let me know how much she actually cared. Her comments were that "your writing will get better with time" and that it is important to write about things that are close to us. This advice has stuck with me throughout my entire life, and I owe a tremendous amount of my writing abilities to her. Thank you professor for all your hard work and feedback. It meant the world.

Defeated could not be any closer to home. I am a football coach and teacher at a middle school in New Haven. I am married and have a daughter. *Defeated* is a novel. It is fiction, but at the same time, it is more real than I could have ever imagined. When I first started writing *Defeated,* it was just a way to vent out my feelings about the world around me. To process my life as a coach, my marriage, and the birth of my daughter. I then thought about the lives of my students and players and their day to day struggles that they hide so tragically well. Their names are changed, but their battles have not. They continue to fight each and every day against insurmountable odds. My heart goes out to them grinding through a world I will never know.

The biggest concern in launching *Defeated* out into the world is how it would impact those I care about. The problems, situations, and circumstances are so real and they may offend those I care about or at least shine a light onto the intimate moments of my life. There is some anxiety in that process that I am still not totally comfortable with, and probably never will be, but this is my story. The good, the bad, and everything in between. I tried to be as honest as possible about retelling the snapshots and moments that stuck with me. Without struggle there can be no progress, and without progress there can be no accomplishments.

I want to thank the most important person in my life: my mom. She was the type of person they talk about in fairy tales; someone so nice, so compassionate, so selfless, that it seems impossible for someone like that to exist, but I had the privilege of having that person as my mother. She taught me to treat others with respect and compassion above all else. She taught me the value of sticking by your family and loving them with all your heart. Her time on this earth was taken way too short, but her impact on those who knew her was far from it. I love you, mom. Thank you for all you did for me and our family.

I want to thank my dad for all he has done for me. He helped pay for my education, took care of two boys to the best of his ability, while still working over forty hours a week and suffering from three back operations, and a neck surgery. He is someone I admire for his consistent work ethic and positive disposition. He loved my mom with all his heart, and that love never has gone away and never will. If I can be half the man he has become then I have done alright in this life.

I want to thank my wife, Sarah. *Defeated* chronicles personal moments between us, and they are not easy to think about, and even harder to write about. She is a fantastic mother and she will always own a special place in my heart for as long as I live.

I want to thank my daughter, Nora. I do not know much about this existence, but I do know that nothing is more rewarding than seeing her grow. Her curiosity, smile, and energy make life worth living. I love you. Please keep being your crazy, silly self.

Lastly, I want to thank you, the reader. You picked up this book and gave it a chance, which is all I can ask. Maybe you get something out of it, or maybe it becomes a paper-weight, but the fact you took the time to invite this story into your life means everything to me. It has been a dream of mine to put my name on the cover of a book, to call myself an author, and to tell my story. Thank you for giving me that opportunity. Thank you for giving me that chance.

Chapter 1
The Game

Thirty-five seconds left. For most people, it was 35 seconds left in the middle school championship game, and that was it, but for Coach V and the Cougars, it meant more than that. It meant that hard work and dedication could lead to success. It meant that banding together and supporting each other through tough times worked. It meant that success was not by accident, but a loss made all those clichés, pep talks, and practices useless. A loss made it mean nothing at all.

The pressure was on Coach V to dial up the right play to bring home the championship. He searched his play chart, which was one double-sided laminate paper with Cougars written on top along with a picture of a clipart cougar flexing his arms.

Terrell trotted over. He was the quarterback on the team. A tall well-built, dark skinned kid with hair that puffed up like a mushroom. He was soft-spoken, but forceful when he needed to be. Coach said jump and he soared. He was fast, athletic, and smart. He was one with potential.

Terrell would normally ask "what's the play?" But this was too big a moment, and he knew Coach was already showering his chart to find the play that could get them a championship.. The whole offense was formed in a horseshoe-shaped huddle. Sweat and dirt covered their bright yellow uniforms and torn-up white pants. They took turns squirting water into their mouths, as they breathed deeply in and exhaled powerfully out. No one said a word, and all that could be heard were the breaths of 11 kids scared out of their minds of what was to happen next.

"Listen," Coach began, and all eyes began to focus on his. Coach could feel a collective weight in his next words, and he knew he needed to choose them carefully, for they could very well decide the fate of the game.

"We need to pass here. There's only 35 seconds left, and we have no more time outs. They are going to expect it, so it's got to be perfect," Coach said pointing at the chest of Terrell.

Terrell nodded his head slightly.

"Lito, you need to run that post. Ten yards hard to the outside, then bust your ass inside. The safety will cheat up and that's when you'll hit 'Em."

Lito was just a smidge taller than Terrell, but was easily the best player in the whole city. He was strong, fast, had incredible hands, and could hit with the best of them. He was one of the few that could do this on a higher level if he stayed out of trouble.

Lito was also dark-skinned, but had short buzzed hair. He spoke with more slang than Terrell and had a bit more rebellion to him. It wasn't that he didn't follow orders, just that he liked to do things his own way. The big question with Lito was could he buckle down and focus in the big moments when the team was counting on him?

"I gotcha coach," Lito said, twirling his mouthpiece in his hand.

"Vinny, you run the fly like your life depends on it. If you get the separation, T will let it rip to you."

Vinny was a lanky but deceivingly strong kid. He had curly jet-black hair and dark eyes. He had olive skin and big hands. He was one of, if not the fastest players on the team.

"Got you, Coach," Vinny said as he strapped his helmet."

"Freddy, I need you to block first, then run that slant pattern, you got me?"

Freddy was average height, average build. He had white skin and brown eyes. He always had a look of bewilderment, you were not totally sure if the lights were on and if anyone was home, but Freddy was always giving max effort which is all you can ask.

"You got it, Coach."

"Gentlemen, this is the moment we've been waiting for... the moment we've practiced for all summer, why we've run all those snakes, why we've hit each other's lights out in practice. Let's go out there and give it all we've got. Don't leave nothing back. You hear me?"

"Yes, Coach," some of the team responded weakly.

"I said, do you hear me?"

"Yes! Coach!"

"Then, let's get after it then. Family on 3! 1, 2, 3!

"Family!" They all shouted as they broke the huddle and hustled to the line of scrimmage for the final play of the year.

Chapter 2
Mr. V to Coach V

It started like any other morning for Mr. V. He woke up reluctantly, hitting his alarm snooze twice to gain a pointless 20 minutes of extra rest. It was actually pretty ironic how just as he could feel sleep coming his alarm would go off again. He thought about using this analogy to describe irony to his class. He managed to add it to the notepad on his phone.

He considered a shower and shave. He was already running late and didn't have the energy. Instead, he took some wipes from the bathroom and scrubbed his essential parts, then sprayed his chest and neck with body spray. That'll do for today.

Mr. V brewed some coffee with his Keurig and heated up a microwave burrito while his coffee was brewing. They tasted pretty good for being picked out by his wife, and as a result gluten free and low in sodium. Once his coffee was ready he added his two sugars and then went into the bedroom to kiss his wife goodbye on the forehead. It was a tradition that started for as long as they had been married, which was now 4 years, which kind of took him by surprise when he really thought about it.

He got in his 2007 Chrysler Sebring Convertible, which wasn't very practical for the harsh New England weather, and certainly not reliable with over 170,000 miles, but he was fully fine with anything as long as it got him where he needed to go.

The ride to his school wasn't too far; about twenty minutes give or take some light traffic. Mr. V lived in a sub-urb of Fairfield County, one of the wealthiest counties in the entire United States. However, his annual salary of $40,000 a year wouldn't raise many eyebrows. But that's what they tell you when you get into teaching. He remembered several of his college professors saying flat out, "there isn't any money in education, so don't get in it for that." At the time, he was taken back by the older professor for being so blunt, but looking at it now, he couldn't help but feel at least a little glad that someone had the stones to tell it like it was.

But, this was the path he chose. A teacher. A middle school teacher in New Haven, Connecticut. New Haven is known for 3 things: Yale, pizza, and crime. It got rated the 4th most dangerous city in the entire United States this year. Just behind cities like Detroit, Flint, and Compton. Not ex-actly good company. There were many situations they didn't teach you in college. Forget designing lessons or units, or assessing student work, what do you do when a student stabs someone with a pencil? Or has their head down refusing to wake up after 45 minutes? Or won't surrender a cell phone responding only with "you ain't taking nothing!" Situations they didn't exactly train you for in school, but maybe they should have.

Luckily, Mr. V fared better than most. He was the third English teacher the school had hired in three straight years. The first teacher quit after three months because she couldn't deal with the stress and aggravation from the kids, along with the constant workload. Rumor has it she spent night after night crying from the stress. The next teacher was a tattooed bald guy named Nemo. He made it a whole year but then realized this wasn't the job for him. He had a band on the side and didn't want to dedicate the time to grade papers, prepare lesson plans, and deal with the behaviors. As the year ended, he told the staff he was calling it quits and they began the search for a 3rd new teacher. They wanted someone brand new - a male, they could mold into a future teacher, and they landed on a candidate. It was Mr. V., a fresh out of college bright-eyed bushy-tailed, twenty-three-year-old who was eager to find a job as a teacher.

Mr. V pulled off the highway and made his way to a red-light intersection. There was an abandoned gas station on his left, and a boarded-up foreclosed house to his right. A McDonald's was just up ahead in the distance, sandwiched in between two rundown homes with peeled grey paint, and chipped wood. Mr. V had made this drive for three years straight but couldn't help but be a bit paranoid. Nothing had ever happened, just strange homeless people walking by with shopping carts, casually dressed high school or college students walking past with headphones glued to their ears, or cell phones securely in their hands. He knew there was nothing to worry about, yet he continued to scan left and right, side to side, anticipating impending danger that never seemed to arrive.

The light turned green, and Mr. V bolted a right-hand turn toward Merit School. The school was beautiful. It was built ten years ago. It had had these large clear windows a prestigious looking gold sign on the side of the red brick that read "Merit Middle School," and flags of every country that hung in the doorway. Each class had a SMART board, and at least 3-4 computers, which depending on your luck, could be in good shape.

Mr. V made his way to the office to check the big board. It was filled with all the staff who would be out for the day. Sometimes the entire board was covered with names, and times, and the people covering. It looked like an impossible math equation that Stephen Hawking would need help to solve. Mr. V hated to call out for a couple of reasons: one being he hated creating sub work, another was he hated being behind on his classes--there was so much to do and one day could throw the whole marking period off, but the last was he simply did not want the reputation of being a slacker. Sure, there were days where he'd prefer to stay in bed and play video games, or watch TV, or just have a mental health day to catch up on grading or other lesson plans, but it wasn't worth it. Mr. V. wanted to be a good teacher, wanted to be dependable, and that required being there even when you didn't want to be.

Mr. V made his way through the halls to the copy machine and began to make copies of today's material. The classes were writing narratives, and he was stressing the importance of sensory details, which were like a foreign language to most of them or they didn't care, but most likely it was a combination of both.

Usually, making copies was like playing a game of Russian Roulette. It would overheat, jam, or just be out-of-service. Many days, Mr. V had lost battles with the copier, but, today, it spit out 100 copies without an issue, which was a good start.

He took the papers and went to his desk, to check emails. There were the usual BS emails about staff fundraisers, books for sale, or reminders of due dates and meetings. Nothing important as usual.

Mr. V drank his coffee in peace, as he enjoyed his few minutes of quiet because he knew all too well how it would change.

His first period class. They were okay, a little hyper, but manageable. Freddy was the one who really stuck out to him. Amongst a school filled in latino and black students, Freddy was a blonde-haired, blue-eyed, short stubby kid. He had freckles under his eyes and spoke in an aw-shucks way that it was hard not to find adorable. Freddy was lazy as sin though. Most of the time, he just sat there staring at the wall, or floor. He wasn't poorly behaved like some of the class, but he did little to no work, and it was impossible to see what he knew. Was he stupid? Was he a genius? Did he understand and just simply not want to try? Or was he just clueless? All impossible questions to answer. No parent had ever come to report card conferences or meet-the-teacher night, which was, sadly, rather common. They would be lucky if they filled up a classroom of twenty parents out of over a hundred students.

"How's it going, Freddy?" Mr. V asked, nudging him on his shoulder.

Freddy shrugged, "Good." he managed to spit out after a long pause.

"You want to give this a try? What are some things you can smell or taste or see in your story?"

Freddy was silent, rubbing his chin for an answer.

"I'm not sure..."

"Hmm, where does your story take place?"

Again, a long pause, followed by more chin rubbing.

"You have an idea for a story, right?"

"Not yet," he responded quickly this time.

"Come on Freddy, we need an idea to get out there. That was due weeks ago." Mr. V said, throwing his hands in the air.

"Think about some tough choice or challenge you have had to overcome and just write about it. You can do it. I know you can."

Freddy nodded and picked up his pen. Mr. V took that as a sign to move along, so he did.

Mr. V made his way around the rest of the class and checked on a couple of other students' work. Some were starting to make some progress, being specific about the type of things they saw. He praised the students who were describing the beach and used details like "slimy, sticky sea water" or "wet smelly bathroom floor." He begged students who wrote sand and hot dogs, to go a little further to describe how the hot dogs tasted, and how the sand felt? Some responded well, nodding and continuing to write, while others shrugged their shoulders, and some didn't write at all.

He made his way back to Freddy before class ended, hoping he had completed something. He noticed on Freddy's paper there was just a bunch of circles and doodles. Nothing inappropriate, but nothing worthwhile. Mr. V pulled up a seat next to Freddy.

"I need some work, bud." Mr. V began in a quiet, understanding tone. He tried to be as heartfelt and serious as possible without sounding too over the top.

"You are failing my class, and it seems like you don't really care…"

He glanced over at Freddy hoping to see some sort of reaction, but all he got was a blank stare and more doodles on the paper.

"I think you have a lot of potential bud; I just need you to let it out. Can you do that Freddy?"

Freddy managed to nod slightly. It wasn't exactly a ringing endorsement, and Mr. V had tried this talk before, yet the results were the same. No work from Freddy. No success.

The bell rang and class had ended. Students exited in their usual aggressive way, piling out the doorway like cattle making their way to the feeding line. Freddy picked up his

17

stuff and followed in a casual motion with a student from class. Mr. V overheard some conversation about Call of Duty and the graphics or gameplay or something like that, but it was too far in the distance to clearly make it out.

Mr. V had a break and decided to make his way down to the principal's office. It was time to talk about Freddy. He called home at least 3 times and the number was out of service. Mom or dad never showed up to a conference, and he had run out of ideas. It was time to ask for reinforcements.

He hated going to the principal's office and he rarely did. He preferred to keep his head down at all costs. Never bring attention to yourself unless you need to, but, now in his 3rd year, he had a pretty good relationship with her. She was a sweet lady. She was from Nicaragua and got her master's in psychology. Some of the teachers called her pillow because she was really soft on punishing the kids, but Mr. V stayed away from all of that talk. She was always fair to him, sticking up for him when parents challenged his methods, giving him positive reviews on his yearly evaluations, no she was not someone he wanted to let go by the wayside, especially, when he heard about so many other teachers hating their principals and wanting to escape for dear life.

He carefully made his way to her office and noticed the secretary on the phone. Mr. V mouthed to her "Dr. D available?" and she nodded and gave a thumbs up. Mr. V walked slowly to the door which had a window that you could see through. There was clearly someone she was talking to, but he couldn't tell for sure. Mr. V was about to turn around and leave when she waved him in. He was surprised and pointed at himself as if to say "me?" she nodded, and he began to panic. What had happened now? She never wanted to speak to him unless it was something bad. Who was in there? What was he being accused of? All sorts of thoughts raced around his head.

"Mr. V. Just the person I wanted to see."

Dr. D wore conservative, yet well-fitting, clothing. High. tight skirts that flattered her frame, which wasn't half bad for a woman in her mid-sixties. She had thick rimmed glasses and spoke with a Spanish accent that at times fluttered her words together, but it was always easy to understand her.

"Sorry for bothering you, Dr. D..." Mr. V was kicking himself. He should have stayed upstairs and enjoyed his prep. Why did he stick his neck out and get himself in this mess?

"No, no your timing is great actually. You know Coach Bryant?"

Mr. V forgot all about the visitor in the corner of the room, hidden in the doorway, which was surprising because he was massive. A 6-foot 4 large black man, with a heavy beard and a wide body. He had tattoos all over his forearms and rings on almost every finger.

"How's it going Coach?" Mr. V said, extending his hand.

Coach leaned in his chair and extended his hand to meet Mr. V's. It practically took over his hand making it nearly invisible.

"We have some troubling news Mr. V…."

Again, his mind raced about all the possibilities. He couldn't think of anything he said to a student that was inappropriate, or anything on Facebook he posted that would get him in trouble, no late nights out at the bar where he got too drunk and ran into a parent or faculty member. So why was he so damn nervous?

"As you know Coach Bryant has been with us for over ten years now. He is a staple of our school and has had a tremendous amount of success with the football team and the Boys and Girls Club."

Mr. V nodded his head but still couldn't see where this was going. Each sentence dragged on, and it felt like an eternity for Dr. D to spit out what she was trying to say. If it was off with his head, he wanted to know already.

"Coach Bryant has just received word of an opportunity in Springfield. He would be doing similar work as he does here, but he would be closer to his mother and father who are not feeling so well lately."

Mr. V found it odd that Dr. D was telling him all this. For one, Coach never had trouble speaking for himself. He spoke frequently when Mr. V was walking his class around the school, in the mornings after breakfast, or on the way to gym or music, or after lunch. He attempted to walk them in a single file line with limited talking, but these are 12 to 13-year-old kids, and that was nearly impossible. He would carry on conversations for an extended period of time, sometimes too long to the point where Mr. V had to stop him politely and bring his class upstairs to get started with class and make sure no-one was getting into fights are causing problems. He didn't mind it though because deep down he knew the longer the kids saw that Mr. V was friendly, perhaps even friends with, a six-foot four, two hundred and eighty-pound black man, then maybe they would look differently at the blonde haired blue-eyed white boy from the suburbs, who was one hundred and eighty pounds soaking wet and far from intimidating.

"Congrats, Coach, that's awesome. It will be sad to see you go, and I'm sure some of the boys will be upset."

Coach nodded, "Thanks, It's gonna be tough to leave, but I gotta do it."

There was a long pause. The anticipation built in the room as collectively everyone tried to break the silence, but no one knew what to say.

"Certainly, you will be missed Coach, for sure," Dr. D said, finally breaking up the silence.

"But, that brings us to you. I remember you saying you wrestled in high school. Is that correct?"

Mr. V was taken aback by the question as it was more direct than usual from Dr. D. It was such a minute detail on his resume and an even smaller conversation point with Coach Bryant.

"Yes, that's true."

Mr. V felt the need to severely downplay his athletic success, which was indeed limited. He wrestled for four years, and he was about as average a player as you could ask for - average footwork, size, speed, hands, technique. His best skill was luck more than anything.

He was nothing compared to Coach Bryant though. Bryant was ranked as a top-five recruit coming out of high school, his parents moved to Texas to give him more notoriety and a chance at landing a big time scholarship. It worked. He got a full ride to the University of Virginia, playing with the likes of Michael Vick and the draft a real possibility. Then, on one out of thousands, he left his feet for an interception, jumping as high as he always had, arms outstretched as they've done countless times as well. The ball landed in his grasp when he heard a loud "pop" and felt a deep burning sensation in his knee. The pain was indescribable, and he couldn't even lift his leg. Trainers came pouring onto the field shaking their heads as he was carted off the field along with his dream of the NFL.

"Oh, I see, well let me explain our predicament here..." Dr. D continued.

"We take great pride in our football team here. It has been a staple of the school and the community, and we would hate to see it go."

Mr. V nodded along politely.

"We were wondering if you had any interest in coaching our football team for this upcoming season?"

Mr. V took those words in and digested them. He wanted to ensure he responded carefully, respectfully, and accurately. He knew football, but no more than the average sports fan. He couldn't be a coach.

"Wow, I am honored you would offer me that opportunity, but, I... I'm not sure I am qualified..."

"It would be temporary until we can find a suitable candidate." Dr. D quickly retorted.

"Um, I don't know…"

"V, listen…" Coach Bryant interrupted.

"I gotta be honest here. The boys need football. It kills me to leave, but I have to be there for my mom and dad. I know it's a lot to take in all at once, but we really need someone, and the season starts in two weeks."

He shrugged his shoulders and put his hands across his chest.

Mr. V had a lot of questions and red flags that told him not to do this. He had a wife at home that he already did not see as often as he liked. He had piles and piles of papers he neglected to grade, he had little time to go to the gym and get his body back into the image he preferred, and he was not sure how he could control 25 kids from New Haven or get them to listen and learn. Oh, and he never coached football, let alone played.

"So what do you say?" Coach Bryant asked.

Right then and there he should have said no, walked away, shook their hands, and gotten on with his day, but he didn't. Maybe, he didn't want to let Coach Bryant and Dr. D down. Maybe he felt bad for the kids and them having no team this year, but more than likely he was too scared to say no despite all the reasons he had to do so.

***

Six months ago on a cold winter morning.

It felt like any other day. He woke up after a decent night's sleep, drank his coffee, took his vitamins, and then quickly changed and went to the gym. Shortly into his workout, Rachel sent him a text to "return home as soon as he could." He asked her if he was okay and she responded "yes, I just need to talk to you." Coach began to panic. He thought about what could have happened, or what was so urgent. He was faithful to her, he didn't break anything, so what was going on that was such a big deal?

He gathered his gym bag quickly and almost ran to his car. It was a leg day; he wouldn't forget that because his hamstrings and calves stung after every step, even after a modified, shortened workout. He returned home and walked up the front porch practically shaking with fear at what was in store for him.

There was Rachel, standing right in the middle of the kitchen. She had her hands behind her back and tears in her eyes.

"Baby, what's going on? Are you okay?"

She could not speak and she didn't even try to. All she could do was nod her head, place her arms in front of her, and reveal what was in her hands.

It was a small tube that looked like a thermometer.

He leaned in to get a closer look as It read pregnant across in big black letters.

Chapter 3
Freddy

"**D**ouble Kill," Freddy screamed to himself. He saw the terrorist's head explode and crimson red filled the screen.

He was on a roll, registering 15 kills and only one death. His weapon of choice was the AK-47, along with the last stand perk, and double tap.

Freddy was sitting on a pillow on the floor with a flat - screen TV hugged against the wall. He had an Xbox One console on the floor with wires and cables tangled all over the place. He loved his Xbox One. Every day at school he dreamed of coming home and playing it and waking up all he thought about was playing it all day. How many kills could he get? Could he rank up to the top 100 in the world? His goal was to be one of the best and he thought he was well on his way.

"What are you doing?" It was Freddy's older brother Chase. A long haired well-built high school sophomore. He spoke with a deep raspy voice that didn't quite match his appearance.

"Just a couple more rounds, then I'll get ready. I swear." Freddy begged.

"Nope, get your stuff together we are leaving in five minutes."

Freddy thought about fighting back, arguing about how this wasn't fair, but it was no use. He was no match for his brother.

Freddy shared a room with his brother, well not just a room, a mattress on the floor, and a dresser. The top three drawers were his brothers and the bottom two were his. Freddy quickly grabbed a new pair of underwear, his jeans, an undershirt, and his blue polo shirt for school. He laced up his Reebok sneakers and headed toward the door.

"Your book bag?" his brother asked with his hands up in the air.

Freddy turned back and found it right next to the pillow where he was sitting down just a moment ago.

Freddy walked through the bitter cold streets of New Haven with his backpack over one shoulder, and his hood over his head. It didn't nearly offer enough warmth as his ears still burned with the sting from the cold. His hands were in the pocket of his hoodie, but that did little to protect them from the harsh 30-degree weather and periodic wind that violently attacked him. He thought about how strange the weather was. It was so cold in these October mornings and had the tendency to warm up radically in the afternoon. His brother walked slightly ahead of him, securely carrying his backpack on both his shoulders. He wore his varsity football jacket and a skull cap on his head, which still allowed for some of his long hair to slip through the sides.

Freddy was freezing. He hated school, hated the walk, hated his classmates, hated the teachers, hated having to sit there and listen to stupid nonsense, especially when he could be there playing COD on his Xbox, slaying noobs, and improving his skill.

Freddy smiled with those thoughts circling in his head when his brother's outstretched arm stopped him at an intersection.

"Keep your damn head up," his brother said with an aggravated look on his face.

Freddy often made mental errors like that, losing track of where he was or what he was doing. He didn't do it on purpose, but for some reason he just always found himself staring out and then getting in trouble in school or having to get an earful from his mom or brother. He didn't like it, but he didn't know how to stop it either.

"Alright, we are here, " his brother said with a sigh of relief.

It was Merit school, a large brick building with beautiful windows all around, surrounded by abandoned buildings and low-income housing apartments.

"Do some work today, and stay out of trouble. You hear me?" his brother said pointing at him.

Freddy nodded.

"I said – do you hear me?"

"Yah," Freddy managed to say.

His brother watched Freddy as he walked through the large steel doors into school, and then turned and walked away running ten minutes late for homeroom.

Freddy's first period class was Mr. V's Language Arts class. It wasn't all bad. It could be boring from time to time, but Freddy appreciated how Mr. V talked about video games and movies. Freddy was bugging Mr. V to give him his gamertag so they could play online. Mr. V kept saying "maybe, if you do some work I'll give it to you."

Freddy was inspired to do some work in that very moment. He looked at his paper and saw the heading "Sensory Details" which stated, "create 5 sensory details for each sense: sight, smell, sound, taste, and feel." Freddy had a problem; he didn't even have an idea for a story. He tried, but any time he tried to brainstorm an idea like Mr. V showed him, but anytime he thought of something it left just as quickly as it came.

So he just sat there thinking of something anything, but his brain was failing him. He picked up his pen

but they vanished into thin air just as quickly.

Mr. V was right in front of him and he could see the light on his face. Mr. V had a look of expectation as if he was going to see something glorious, something unbelievable.

"How'd you do?" Mr. V asked peeling away Freddy's hands to clearly see the paper sitting flat on the desk.

Freddy could feel the disappointment ooze out of Mr. V. All that enthusiasm burst into utter disappointment, shame, and guilt. Freddy wanted so badly to explain himself, to open up his mind let Mr. V see how he had tried, how he really tried, but it wasn't working for him. It was a maze he couldn't find his way through, getting trapped into corner after corner each time.

But Freddy didn't do that. He just sat there looking down at the doodles that were supposed to be well thought out ideas. He listened to Mr. V tell him that he needed to call home, and how he believed in him, and how he could do better. Freddy took all the comments in, but despite the pep talk he knew it would be no use. No matter what anyone said Freddy was not going to get it. He knew he would scrape by on the mercy of the teachers, or the fact they didn't want to deal with him anymore.

Mr. V gave him a pat on the shoulder when he concluded his speech, and the bell rang almost instantly after. Freddy lethargically gathered his books and papers and shoved them into his backpack. It was a mess and Freddy knew it, but he didn't have the desire to organize it, or the know-how for that matter.

The rest of the day went on like normal. Science and Social Studies weren't that difficult. It was a lot of notetaking, a lot of copying terms, and Freddy sat in the back, so it was easy for him to doodle drawings, or signs and have the teacher think he was simply following along.

Lunch came and Freddy sat at his usual table with the rest of the football team. Freddy remembers the first day of school where he thought about where to sit and he began to panic. His only friend Jeremiah had a different lunch , and he scanned the whole room and had no idea who he could sit near. There was nothing more humiliating than sitting alone. No one would say anything, but the judgment, the stares, the whispers; Freddy already stood out being one of three white kids in a school otherwise filled with Spanish and blacks. He didn't need the extra ammunition for a bully.

Freddy thought fast and made his way to a table with 5 to 6 open spots. He slid in quietly and put his lunch down on the table, hoping for dear god that no one would say "Hey you!" or "What do you think you're doing?" Freddy just quietly sat there quietly picking up the fake rib sandwich smothered in BBQ sauce and ate it. It tasted like plastic with cheap BBQ sauce on top, but Freddy kept eating, small bite, after small bite. He didn't dare look up and didn't dare stop, so he just kept eating. He caught a couple of the group's comments. Conversations about last night South Park and some of the girls in school, mildly interesting topics that he could envision himself participating in, but right now was not the time nor the place.

Freddy finished his lunch right before the bell rang and students slowly got up to go in their perspective lines. The rest of the day flew by. Math class was a bore. Freddy just put his head down and slept through the entire thing. The teacher at times would nudge him to wake up, but a lot of the time he left him alone and Freddy woke up at the sound of the bell.

When school was over Freddy made the mile walk back home. His brother had football practice so he had to do it on his own. Freddy hated the walk home. There were always loud older kids shouting things in a large group, high fiving, screaming, dancing, or just standing there in a massive circle. Homeless men were sitting on corners with signs asking for help, and others that would nudge him and ask for change. Freddy learned the perfect strategy; just keep your head down and walk. He walked at a steady pace, not too fast where he'd overexert himself, but not too slow where he'd attract attention, and his strategy had worked for him so far.

The walk always seemed like hours, but in reality, it took him less than 20 minutes. His building was on the corner of Grant and Edgewood, and anytime he told people that they started to cringe. He wasn't sure exactly why. He had seen some shady characters, had heard some gunshots, but nothing too strange. As he was walking up the stairs to the main apartment door two black men quickly ran down the stairs opposite him. They kept their heads down and raced down the stairs in a hurry. Freddy quickly took the key from his pocket and opened the main apartment building door. Then very quickly he made his way up two staircases to the 3rd floor and opened the door. Immediately Freddy turned the lock on the door handle and the lock up top. Finally, he was home.

It was the usual routine for Freddy. He threw off his backpack right at the door and ran to the fridge. It was as bare as usual with a large bottle of coke in the center, some left over McDonald's in a white bag, and a half gallon of milk. Freddy grabbed the milk and Captain Crunch on top of the fridge and poured himself a bowl. It was delicious. His favorite part was when the milk at the end where all the little remnants of the cereal were left over and he could just slurp it all up.

Freddy finished his cereal and then put the empty bowl in the dishwasher with about five others. He didn't feel like doing dishes yet but he knew he'd have to before his brother got home. That was one of his jobs, dishes, taking out the trash, and picking up after himself. His brother always got on him for that one.

Freddy booted up his Xbox and already had the chills. This was what he waited for all day. He loved being able to sit on the pillow on his floor with the TV in front of him, controller in hand, and just play.

He could remember just a year ago how his mother surprised him last Christmas with an Xbox. She had asked him what he wanted and when he said it she smiled and told him how expensive it was and how she couldn't afford it. Freddy couldn't help but sulk. He wanted to experience the graphics, the awesome games. He wanted it all. And sure enough, when Christmas came there it was. His own personal Xbox. Freddy kissed his mom, hugged her, he thanked her again and again. He was so happy to have her as a mom, she was the best.

Hours passed by and Freddy's brother should be home any minute. Practice was over and he would expect the trash out, the dishes done, and the place picked up. Freddy panicked; he didn't want to feel the wrath of his brother. He never laid a hand on him, but he had a way to make his voice sharper and speak in an abrupt way that it pierced through Freddy's heart.

Freddy was about to get up when he heard the door creak open.

This was it--he was screwed. He slacked off too much, played too much Xbox and had to face the music.

But Freddy was surprised when the door did finally pry open it was his mom, not his brother. His mother put her hand on the door frame to keep her balance and took slow methodical steps.

She was wearing her usual clothes. A New York Giants hoodie and baggy black sweatpants. Her hair was up in a bun, and her face was as white as a ghost's.

Freddy got up and quickly made his way to the door like always when his mom came home.

"You need help Ma?"

His mom's eyes open, but unfocused. They scanned the room unable to stay locked on one target for too long.

"No, I'm fine," she managed to say while waving her right hand, her left was still glued to the door frame.

Freddy took three big steps back not offering help but being there just in case she fell.

His mother let go of the frame and began to move, she moved slowly in a herky-jerky motion, side to side, more like a waltz moving left and right versus side to side. She managed to stabilize herself when she felt herself veering too far to one side. She made it about four feet ahead when she lost her balance on Freddy's pillow and tumbled to the ground. Luckily she was able to put her hands out to brace herself, but it was a violent fall with a sickening thud. Freddy did all he could to try and help her, but she fell so fast he couldn't react in time. He felt so bad. He should have been there to help her. Why didn't he help her?

Freddy raced to her side and placed his hand on her bicep and tried to get her back up.

"I'm sorry mom. I should have helped you it's my fault."

Freddy felt an arm on his shoulder and quickly turned around. It was his brother, sweaty with his lettermen's jacket on and his football pants covered in dirt.

"Grab one side and let's lift her."

Freddy got on the right and his brother went on the left.

"On three: one, two, three."

They picked her up as they had done a couple times before. Usually, his mother could make it to the bedroom on her own, but there were times she couldn't do it, and this was one of those times.

Freddy looked at his mother; her head hunched down and her body limp and almost lifeless. She was difficult to carry, even though she didn't weigh a lot.

His brother took a deep breath then exhaled.

"Let's put her down here."

They carefully laid her down on the mattress on the floor. She landed on her butt first and Freddy and his brother guided her slowly down to the pillow. Her eyes were closed as soon as her head hit the pillow.

Freddy's brother put his ear right up against his mother's lips. He kept it there for a good five seconds before pulling back.

"What'd you do that for?" Freddy asked.

"Don't worry about it, you better get to work cleaning this place. I'll get dinner started."

Freddy grabbed a roll of paper towels and started to wipe. There were stains on the sofa and pillows, Freddy did the best he could but some of the stains were so deep that no matter how hard he pressed it couldn't be removed. He kept at it though and did the best he could.

"Dinner's ready," his brother said and Freddy quickly rose to his feet and made his way to the small dinner table. It was a card table with a white plastic tablecloth laid over. They replaced it every now and then because the stains accumulated, and by the looks of the red and brown stains covered all across the tablecloth, it was time to find a new one soon.

Freddy's brother scooped some pasta from the bowl and placed it on his dish.

"Pasta again!"

Freddy's brother was about to place the dish in front of him but quickly brought it back to his chest. Almost like a pump fake in basketball.

"Don't want it? Fine, starve."

Freddy shook his head, "No, no, I'm sorry."

Freddy's brother finally placed the dish in front of him and Freddy ate. The pasta was warm, the sauce tasted like ketchup, it was very watery and flavorless. The pasta was in big clumps and it was hard for Freddy to chew because it got caught in his teeth or the roof of his mouth.

It was dead silent while they ate. Just chewing, drinking, and the clanging of the plastic on the paper plates.

"How was practice?" Freddy asked, putting a fork fill of past in his mouth.

There was a pause. Freddy's brother glared at him as if he was debating whether or not it was worth it to respond.

"Okay, coach is up our ass. We need to win the next two games or we aren't going to the playoffs."

Freddy nodded. There was another silence that continued to build.

"After you are done eating you need to clean up and do your homework."

Freddy nodded as they finished the rest of their dinner in silence.

Freddy threw the plates in the garbage and put the plastic silverware in the dish bucket. He rinsed out the large pan that the pasta was cooked in and made sure all the trash was thrown away.

Luckily Freddy's brother never really checked his homework or paid much attention to whether it was done or not, so when he finished cleaning he could squeeze in a couple games before bed.

Freddy booted up the Xbox when he heard a loud banging at the door. Freddy froze. He quickly muted the TV and then didn't move a muscle. His brother charged in the room and put his finger over his mouth as if to say, "shut up!"

Freddy's brother picked up a bat in the corner right near the door.

The knock repeated.

"Who is it!?" Freddy's brother asked.

"Dom the landlord. Open up."

Freddy put down the bat in the corner and removed the locks on the door.

"Your Ma around?" Dom was wearing a sweatsuit that didn't fully cover his large stomach. He had hair that engulfed his body but was bald on top. He was Greek, Italian, or some kind of Spanish. A very unique individual to say the least.

"No, she is out right now... I'm not sure where she is..."

Dom looked at Freddy's brother mysteriously, then at Freddy, then back to his brother.

"Tell her I need to speak with her immediately. Stress to her this is serious. I don't talk to her tomorrow, and we got problems. Understand?"

Freddy's brother nodded. Dom seemed satisfied enough and exited the doorway.

Freddy's brother quickly closed the door and locked everything securely. He took a deep breath, then turned to Freddy.

"Go to bed."

Freddy followed his brother to the bedroom to prepare for bed.

The next morning Freddy followed the normal routine he got up, got dressed, and followed his brother out the door.

On the glass door right before the school entrance, Freddy saw something. It was a black and white flyer that must have been cheaply created on Microsoft Word, with a picture of a clipart football player in the Heisman pose with a would-be tackler at his feet. The flyer read "Football Try-outs Wednesday, September 3rd." Freddy looked at the flyer for a good moment, excited for another season to start. He had hoped maybe this was his year to shine, to be a starter. He was in 8th grade now and he believed that maybe this would be his chance to make an impact. He remembered his brother's first game as a starter. His mom and him in the stands he looked over at her waving at him and clapping her hands. She had a smile beaming on her face and eyes that lit up like he had never really seen before, especially when she looked at him. Freddy wanted that smile again. He wanted to see her clapping, waving, and cheering as he took the field not just as a part of the team, but as a contributor, a starter, and maybe even a captain. Freddy held onto that dream as he walked into school, down the hallway, and toward his homeroom class.

Chapter 4
Practice

Mr. V had taken the job "offer," despite it not really being much of an offer. There were so many reasons for him not to take the job, he could list them off like a grocery list, and the biggest one was Rachel. She was closing in on seven months pregnant by now and he could certainly use the time after school to help set up the nursery and get things together.

Despite all of that though, there was still one really good reason to take the job. It was another reason they couldn't fire him. Not that Mr. V was walking on eggshells; he never got a talk about improving or a scare from the administration that they were paying more attention to him than anyone else, but he still had this feeling of uneasiness. No one came up to him and shook his hand, or wrote him a letter saying how great he was doing. He was kind of in a limbo state that he couldn't shake out of, and it wasn't exactly the most comfortable spot for a third year teacher.

Mr. V had his first practice today after school. He had no idea what to expect or what was in store. There were flyers all over school and all across the neighborhood about this year's team. It could be ten kids, twenty, fifty, or none that came. He had no idea at all.

Mr. V had many different anticipations about what to expect. When he first drove up to the field he realized how different this was. He was expecting a football field equipped with goalposts, lines painted. Instead, it was a barren field half-filled with grass and dirt, a field that was fenced in with grey metal fence, but there was trash engulfed on the outskirts. It looked more like a park to walk your dog, not a place to practice for football.

Mr. V scanned the field from his car. He pretended to fiddle with knobs on the radio and search for things in an effort to pass time. What he really was doing was taking it all in. Parents had lawn chairs off to the side, children climbing trees, and empty water, Gatorade, and Powerade bottles surrounded the outskirts of the field.

Mr. V slowly got out of his car and closed the door. He grabbed his bag and walked up to the field.

It was reassuring beyond words that Mr. V was able to get the recognition from the coach. He felt out of place, to say the least, and getting that simple acknowledgment was worth its weight in gold.

Mr. V scanned the field. From up close the players seemed much smaller. He could almost spot the athletes, the stars right away. They were shirtless, with broad shoulders, and towered over the rest. They were lean but well-toned.

Mr. V thought back to the way he looked in middle school and it was nothing even close to resembling what he saw on the field. If push came to shove, he wondered if he could "take" them in a fight. He had packed on some muscle in his frame, and despite a small belly in his midsection, he was in decent shape. Arms that protruded out, and a chest that did the same. That inner realization gave him the confidence he needed.

Coach V blew his whistle and shouted for the kids to line up across the white line. Luckily, there were lines painted on the field at least. There was a decent turnout of 30 or so kids in a variety of different proportions, heights, weights, and appearances. A mix of Latino and black kids with a variety of different skin tones. Coach V was the only white person on the field along with Freddy.

"My name is Coach V, and I am the head coach of the Cougars." he paused and continued to scan the eyes that looked at him. He was surprised to see all the attention on him. No side conversations, no laughter, very different than when he spoke to his students in class.

"Listen, I am not planning on making cuts. The way I look at it, you will cut yourself. If you work hard, listen, and show me max effort you will have a spot on this team."

He got a couple nods from the eyes staring back at him and some blank stares.

"Who played for this team last year?" three hands shot up casually. A slender looking black kid with short hair. He was about five foot six but carried his weight well. His shirt was off, and he had the start of a six pack. He looked like someone with some athletic ability.

"You, what's your name?"

"Lito," he responded in a confident tone, while his hands were on his sides.

"You start a line right here. What position did you play last year?"

"Running back and linebacker," he responded walking to the spot coach pointed to.

That was good to hear, at least one spot was figured out. He handed Lito a football and he tucked it high and tight in his armpit, the exact way you are coached to hold the football. Coach V nodded approvingly.

"You," he pointed at the next kid who had his hand up. "What's your name?"

"Vinny," he said, in a very soft tone that was barely audible. He was almost six feet tall with long arms and olive skin. He had longer curly hair that he pushed to the side.

"Stand right here," and Vinny jogged over to the spot where Coach was pointing to.

"I like that. From now on we never walk on this field, we jog everywhere is that understood?"

A couple nods scattered throughout.

"I said, is that understood?"

"Yes, Coach!" said almost the entire group in unison. Coach V had a sense of inner pride, that maybe, just maybe he had something here.

"What position did you play last year?" he asked Vinny in a volume only Vinny could hear.

"Wide receiver and corner." He replied, again with that same soft tone.

Coach V nodded and handed him another football. The last hand in the air was Freddy's. Coach V already knew all about Freddy. He was essentially as athletic as a tackling dummy, but he needed someone with a little football experience.

"Okay Freddy, lead this line right here."

Freddy ran to the spot with eager intensity.

"Coach, you are gonna have Freddy be a captain? He sucks!" Lito exclaimed.

Coach V was stunned by the comment. He whipped around and put up his hand.

"Stop! Let me do my job and you just listen." He responded.

"Okay, I am just saying." Lito put his arms up in the air in a gesture that indicated he was willing to give in.

Coach V gave the rest of the players numbers 1, 2, 3 and they broke up into groups for stretches. There were a few kids that had potential, with some athletic ability and quick movements, but they had never touched a football before or even seen a football field.

Not to mention normally a football team has two or three coaches, this was an operation just run by Coach V. He had to teach tackling, blocking, and go over plays all in the span of two weeks. It was overwhelming to say the least.

The team then began to do laps.

The heavier set kids were huffing and puffing, some even had their hands on their heads desperate for air. Some were taking small breaths, and the in shape kids were simply breathing as normal. One kid that towered over Coach V stopped about halfway and started walking.

"Come on big man, keep going, you can do it." Coach thought about him as a solid guard, nose tackle, maybe even offensive tackle if his feet were good enough. After all, you cannot teach size.

The big walked to the end and then fell to a knee then on his back. Coach made his way over, seeing the kid's chest move slowly up and down. That was a good sign. At least he was breathing.

"You alright, big guy?" Coach asked, patting his side.

The kid could only nod his head slightly. He was fine, just very, very out of shape.

"Okay, let's do it again." Coach said and blew his whistle.

Coach turned his back to look at the team and the big fella was already halfway off the field. So much for that.. He thought.

After laps, Coach had the team get water. Many of them were huffing and puffing after only a couple laps. How in the world could he get this team ready to play a football game in two weeks when they couldn't run the field? He was beginning to regret this decision very much.

The team came back from water and formed a straight line in front of Coach.

"Okay, we are going to break into drills. This is the time to show me what you've got. This is a great opportunity for you guys to make an impact…" there were loud noises coming from the side of their field. Coach V watched the player's eyes slowly gravitate past him to something in the distance.

"Hey! Eyes here! Look at me when I am talking." Coach wanted to set the tone. He wanted them to know that he was going to be tough and he needed to be respected.

Many of the eyes returned, which was a good sign he thought. Maybe this wasn't so bad after all. Maybe he would really make a difference. Maybe they would respect him, listen, and become successful.

Then Coach heard a gate slam as 3 teenage boys in masks and backpacks bolted from the store next to the field. They ran right across the field as one of the boys stopped for a second and then took something from his hand and tucked it into his waist. Then he caught up with the rest of the boys as they ran off into the neighborhood well off into the distance.

Sirens started off as whispers grew louder and louder as he had 60 eyes looked quickly at the noise of the sirens, and then quickly turned back toward him. They were looks without fear or concern, just knowing what they were going to do next.

Chapter 5
One Week Before the Game

The first couple days of practice went better than could be expected. The good news was he had found a talented running back. Lito was a strong, tough kid that ran hard and kept his feet moving no matter what. He was one of the fastest players on the team if not the fastest. He ran basic plays with ease. Dives, tosses, blasts. He had great leg strength and a natural ability to glide while he was running in a smooth, seamless motion that looked almost poetic.

He also saw a lot of potential in Vinny. The skinny Latino kid had good feet and great hands. He could catch pretty much everything thrown his way and was fast enough to beat many kids that were going to be lined up across from him, and sometimes if he got a good jump he could beat Lito.

There were some big enough kids who showed some potential that he could plug on the line as well. They took up space, listen for the most part, and were willing to give effort, which is all you could ask.

There was one glaring problem though that was unavoidable. There was no quarterback. A couple kids could throw decent, but they were way too small or had no idea how to play the position.

It was Monday and they only had two full weeks of practice before their first game. He needed someone at quarterback, someone who had a clue, who knew the plays and could at least hand the ball off to Lito.

"Freddy, you are going to be at quarterback today." Coach said. Freddy's eyes beamed as he heard Coach say the words.

"Coach. He sucks." Lito said. He said it so matter-of-factly it caught everyone totally off guard.

"Just shut up and let me coach." Coach didn't know how to handle that situation. It clearly bothered Freddy. He had his head down as he made his way under center.

Practice was beyond difficult. Usually, you had two or three coaches who were able to work with each group. This was a one-man operation, so Coach had to work with the linemen, quarterback, running back, receivers, and defense all at once. It was not hard, it was impossible.

He showed the linemen a stance and told them how to stay low and use their hands to push the guy as far as they could. He worked with Lito on how to hit the right hole on a designated play. Lito knew exactly where to go so coach wasn't too worried about that. Vinny knew how to take handoffs and was a great blocker. His biggest concern was obviously Freddy.

"Freddy, I need you to make sure you understand the plays I give you and execute them right." Coach explained with his hand on his shoulder.

Freddy nodded.

"I just need you to get the ball cleanly to Lito and Vinny. Very basic stuff, but it's gotta be done right and done fast."

Freddy nodded again with some clear nervousness in his eyes.

He then worked with Freddy on how to snap the ball and hand it off to Lito. A basic handoff looks simple, but it takes lots of steps. Freddy was a little robotic, but he knew where the play was going and how to get it there.

"Put the ball here." Lito grabbed the ball and put it right in his stomach with lots of force. It knocked the wind out of Freddy.

"He'll get it. Just give it a little more time. Relax." Coach explained.

Lito visibly rolled his eyes with his hands on his hips.

A couple more plays in and things were looking pretty good. Freddy took a clean snap turned and tossed the ball perfectly to Lito. Lito ran to the outside cleanly and followed a great block by Vinny to go all the way to the end zone.

"Excellent job guys! Great toss, great blocking, and great running!" Coach was very excited. With Lito running and Vinny blocking on the edge he might have something here, depending on how talented other teams were in the district.

"Okay, we are going to try a couple passing plays." Freddy's eyes got wide with excitement.

"We're not going to do this a lot, but we need to have a couple in there just to keep the defense honest."

He remembered Coach Bryant telling him that middle school football was 80% running the ball. Very few teams passed it and if they did, it was short passes with little chance of interceptions or sacks. After all, it was tough to teach kids to block, so having the time to throw was almost impossible. A lot of things had to go right for a pass to work, and it could very easily go wrong.

"Going to call this play-action pass. You are going to fake the toss to Lito to the right and then throw a simple slant route to Vinny over the middle."

Freddy nodded. They broke the huddle and Freddy faked the handoff perfectly, Vinny was wide open but the pass ended up at Vinny's feet. They tried it again and the ball went way over Vinny's head. The third time the ball slipped out of Freddy's hand and the defense picked it up and ran into the end zone.

"Coach, he can't do it," Lito said.

Coach waved the comment off with his right hand.

"We need a quarterback who can throw. We can't run every play."

Lito was beginning to be a pain in the ass, but he was right. Freddy could handle simple handoffs and tosses, but he was clearly nervous and incapable of getting the ball to Vinny.

Coach had the kids take a water break while he thought through his options. Even if other kids could throw they didn't know the plays. He didn't have time to teach them all the basics of quarterback play in two weeks. But if he kept

Freddy in their defenses would stack the line to play the run and Freddy would get killed.

"Coach is there still a spot on the team?" Coach heard Lito's voice and was beginning to get frustrated.

"I don't know, we've got two weeks then we've got a game. I don't know if we've got time to train more players." Coach responded. He turned around and saw a lean black kid a little shorter than Lito with a buzzcut. He was skinny but looked somewhat athletic. He had a physical paper in one hand and a football in the other.

He handed Coach the paper.

"What's your name?" Coach asked.

"Terrell," he said. He then took one step and threw the football in his hand forty yards perfectly downfield to Vinny who was coming back from getting water. The ball twirled in the air with a perfect spiral before landing softly into Vinny's arms.

Coach looked at Terrell who had a confident smile on his face knowing he had impressed.

"Welcome to the Cougars, Terrell."

Chapter 6
First Game

Coach was operating at a consistent pace and fatigue was starting to set in. The routine was waking up at 6 AM, teaching until 3, practice until 5:30, then coming home and supporting his pregnant wife. She was feeling good, which made things easier, but he felt like he was neglecting her and he apologized.

"It's alright," she would say with that smile that always had a way of making him feel better. Her green eyes opening a bit more as she said the words.

"I know you are busy."

He really was. His lesson plans were short and abrupt. He graded papers quickly and with little to no feedback, and he ate quick unhealthy meals that made him tired and bloated.

The good news was the team was looking good. The game was this Saturday and Terrell stepped right in as starting quarterback on Monday. It was hard to put anyone else in at the spot. At the first practice, Terrell took snaps perfectly, got into his drops naturally, and released passes downfield with the slight flick of his wrist.

With Terrell at quarterback, Lito running the ball, and Vinny catching, blocking, and doing the grunt work, they looked ready to be something special. The only problem was Freddy. He could tell that Freddy took the loss of the quarterback job to heart. Coach pulled him aside at the start of Tuesday's practice.

"Look, Freddy, you did a good job, but I have to go with the best guy for the job."

He nodded looking down.

"You are going to be our backup, and starting tight end. We need you this year."

Freddy nodded and then rejoined the team, but it was obvious he was dejected. Coach felt bad, but he knew he had no choice. Putting Freddy out there at quarterback was going to sabotage the entire season, and Terrell had real ability. It wasn't fair to him, or to anyone else.

The rest of the week was spent going over specifics on offense, defense, and special teams.

Defense, they kept really simple. He put four of their biggest kids at linemen and instructed them to go upfield as fast as they could. He mimicked a 3-point stance and told them to get low, fight with your hands, and attack. Some kids looked confused, but he didn't really have time to go over too many specifics. Linebacker was a more important spot so he put both Lito and Vinny at the outside spots with Freddy in the middle. Lots of teams liked to get to the outside so having his best tacklers there helped, and Freddy knew how to read the ball and could at least slow people down. Terrell was placed at safety. He had the instincts and ability to read the whole field so it made a lot of sense. That was pretty much it.

Offense was the biggest thing. Coach had no idea what his opponent was going to bring to the table. The league was broken up into 8 teams. With the top four teams making the playoffs. The team they were playing Saturday was Welsh. It was a notoriously bad school in a very rough neighborhood. He spoke to many of the teachers there and students were consistently getting into fights, skipping class, which made it clear that it was a tough place to teach.

He knew the coach threw staff meetings and functions. He was a nice guy, a tall thin black man with a mini afro. He was the physical education teacher for many years, and well before that, he was a very good high school basketball player in the city. He was soft spoken and was more of a basketball coach than a football one, but his teams were always in the hunt for the playoffs so you couldn't take them lightly.

Coach's plan was simple, a heavy dose of running the ball with Lito in the middle and at the edge, sprinkled in with some quarterback sneaks with Terrell, along with some play-action passes and short passes to Vinny. He wanted the defense to think the ball was only going to Lito, and then hit Vinny with some throws that would catch them off guard.

The week of practice was good. The team looked focused, together, and ready. Even Lito, who had a tendency to talk back, and call people out, was quiet and focused. It was a good sign. Coach brought them together for the huddle on Friday after the walkthrough of practice.

"Listen, our first game is tomorrow, remember to do your jobs, play hard, and we will be fine."

"No, screw that coach, we're winning that thing tomorrow!" Lito exclaimed and the team joined him in hollering. Coach couldn't help but smile as he was excited for how pumped up the team was.

"Okay, family on three, ready.. 1.. 2...3... Family." They all shouted loudly as they broke the huddle for practice.

Many of the students walked home and a couple waited for rides, but Lito hung around with his phone in his hand looking around.

"You need a ride?" Coach asked.

"I'm good, the house is right there, just chillin' for a bit."

He pointed to the neighborhood in the seeable distance. Coach always saw him walk in that direction so he accepted that answer.

"Okay, get a good nights sleep tonight. Good practice today."

He nodded and coach drove off home in the cool fall air.

It was a warm early fall morning as the team packed on the bus to head to the game. The team was all there on time and focused. They reviewed the plays from the week and assignments. He wanted everyone to know what their role was to ensure there was no confusion. There were many kids that were not going to play. He felt bad about that, but when he saw Welsh take the field for warmups he knew that was the right call. They had some big boys, tall, big athletic kids. Nothing too much bigger than what he had, but if some of his younger unathletic kids went on the field there was a chance they were going to get hurt. As a result many of the kids never left the field. Vinny, Terrell, and Lito, for instance, were going to play offense defense and special teams. They were not going anywhere.

The game began with the coin toss. Coach had chosen Vinny, Lito, Terrell, and Freddy as captains. The rest of the team stood in a straight line on the sideline as they watched the four captains get ready for the toss.

"Coach, why'd you make Freddy a captain? He trash," Lito said so the whole team could hear.

"Stop! Focus on the game. We need Freddy, he is important."

The other team's four captains were big stocky kids, with one seemingly athletic kid in the middle. He had braids and a visor across his face mask. Coach could already tell he was going to be a problem.

They had won the toss and were getting the ball first. Coach called a toss play to Lito. On the very first play, Lito took the toss and effortlessly made his way past the line to the edge. He followed a perfect block from Vinny and went all the way to the end zone untouched. The sideline exploded. Coach high fived all the players on the sideline and hugged a couple. What a way to start the season he thought. This is a lot of fun. He padded Lito on the helmet as he came back to the sideline after the touchdown. Vinny lined up for the extra point and nailed it. They were ahead 7-0 on the first play.

Welsh had the ball and they were really sloppy to start. They fumbled their first snap but luckily recovered it. On second down they ran a fullback dive that only got one yard. Third down there was a delay of game penalty and the Welsh coach called a time out to talk to his guys.

"You guys are doing great. Keep up the pressure. Watch the pass. It is 3rd down. Stay with your men and follow the quarterback's eyes."

On third down the athletic kid with the visor tried to take the shotgun snap, but it was well over his head and Freddy dived on the ball. The Cougars got the ball on their 30-yard line in great position to score. Coach jumped up again ecstatic the ball was in their possession, but better yet, it was Freddy who recovered it.

Coach gave Freddy a big hug and explained how proud he was of him.

The first quarter ended as the teams switched ends of the field.

Coach went back to what worked and gave the ball to Lito on a toss. When Terrell dropped back to pitch the ball to Lito, there were defenders closing in, which must have distracted Lito enough to muff the toss. The ball bounced off Lito's hands and trickled around the ground in a crazy manner before a Welsh defender landed on it.

Welsh's offense was very simple. They had their quarterback drop back seemingly to look to pass, and then he would find a hole and run. He was athletic and fast enough to make a bunch of people miss, so it was tough to bring him to the ground. This was the play they ran every single time. Coach screamed for his guys to contain the edge and not let him go to the outside, but that didn't happen. The kid took the snap, dropped back, and found the edge on the right side for a touchdown. The drive took so much time that the Cougars didn't get a chance to get the ball back. The Welsh kicker missed the extra point wide right, and the score was 7-6 at half time.

At halftime, Coach gathered his guys together. "Listen, we're doing okay, we just need to stay focused. We have got to wrap up and bring that quarterback down. Do not let him get to the edge. On offense, we are going to keep running the ball and then hit them with our passing plays. Hey, we are still winning, we are in good shape. "

The team nodded their heads. What coach was beginning to realize was how hard it was to coach a team by himself. He had to watch the players on the field, but also keep a seemingly third eye on the 10-12 kids behind him. They would sometimes ask him questions about the game, or make comments at each other, or even make fun of each other. Coach had to tell them to shut up and focus.

Unfortunately, the second half was the biggest disaster. Their quarterback did exactly what he had done all game. Freddy got through the line and had the kid in his grasp, but simply couldn't bring him down. The quarterback got by

Lito with a swift spin move and then outran Terrell all the way to the end zone on the first play of the second half.

The other sideline erupted, and it was dead silent on their side. Coach clapped his hands and told his guys to stay focused. Many of them were walking off the field, but the other team was going for two. Coach had to use a timeout to stop the play from going on.

"Listen, it is one score, we are fine. Pick your heads up and let's go!"

There was little response. Their eyes looked lost.

The quarterback did the same play he did this time to the opposite side. Luckily Lito was in perfect position and made a great tackle. The two-point try was no good. The score was 12-7

With the ball, Coach went back to Lito on the outside. The Welsh coach smartened up to this strategy. He had the fast quarterback at safety and followed Lito wherever he went. As a result, Lito got little to no yards on the first two carries. Coach then called a quarterback run to Terrell. Terrell was shaking visibly as he took the snap. He rolled out to the right, but the play was designed to go left. Three Welsh defenders were there. He tried to juke them but got nowhere. It was fourth down. Coach called a play-action pass to Vinny. Terrell dropped back and had Vinny open, but the pressure seemed to be too great and he got sacked. Turnover.

The fourth quarter began, and the defense played a little better. They sacked the quarterback on first down, and allowed two short runs, forcing a fourth and short. Luckily for their sake, the Welsh coach called for a passing play when he only needed two yards. The pass was badly underthrown and the Cougars got the ball back. They were going to get the ball back with a chance to go down and score and win.

Coach pulled Terrell aside and told him he needed to throw the ball to Vinny. He would be open, just trust him. Terrell nodded nervously. His hands were shaking. He definitely did not look like the same confident kid that threw the ball that one practice not so long ago.

Coach called the play and Vinny was open. Terrell launched the pass perfectly, but it was just a little too long and despite Vinny's diving effort it fell incomplete.

"Coach, I told you he can't catch!" Terrell said, ripping his helmet off.

Coach was stunned. Terrell never showed that level of disrespect or emotion. He was so even keel. Who was this?

"Coach he can't take his helmet when he's on the field. He has to come off for a play."

"Come here!" Coach yelled.

"You can't do that. Now you have to come off for a play. It was a good pass, just a little wide. It happens."

"Nah, this is bull. He should have had it."

"Freddy, we are going to go blast right with Lito."

Freddy nodded and the team broke the huddle. Freddy fumbled the snap but luckily dove on the ball.

"Grab the freaking ball!" Lito exclaimed, jumping up and clapping his hands wildly in front of Freddy.

"Shut up and play!" Coach shouted from the side.

Technically Terrell could go back in now, but Coach wanted to send a message, plus Terrell was sitting on the bench with his arms lackadaisically stretched across and his head high in the air. If he wasn't begging to go back in why would Coach beg him?

Coach called for a play they only worked on a couple times, a fake handoff to Lito, then a reverse to Vinny. A sort of trick play, but if it worked it had the chance to be a home run. Freddy took the snap, faked the handoff beautifully, so well many of the players followed Lito, except the quarterback. He saw Vinny coming across and stayed with him. Vinny tried to get to the outside, but there was no avoiding him. It was fourth down.

" Terrell come on!" Lito shouted.

"Alright, I'm coming!" Terrell shouted attempting to make his way on the field.

"Woah, woah, where are you going? You can't just go back on the field when you feel like it!" Coach wanted to send the message. He wanted to win the game, but he didn't want to send the message this behavior was tolerable.

"Terrell, Okay, then I quit!" Terrell took off his helmet and slammed it on the ground. He took his shoulder pads and slammed them too.

"Coach! What are you doing? We need him!" Lito shouted.

"He quit. You can join him if you want to," Coach thought it was an empty threat, but sure enough, Lito took off his helmet and followed Terrell to the bench.

Coach was so stunned about what happened that he didn't know what to do. He called a passing play. Moments later, Freddy dropped back and threw a pass right into the arms of a Welsh defender. The kid went 70 yards the opposite direction untouched for a touchdown.

The sideline erupted, as Terrell and Lito left their equipment at Coach's feet.

"Forget this team. Y'all suck."

They then hopped the fence and walked slowly into the distance as the whistle blew signaling the end of the game.

Chapter 7
Coach Ben

Post-game was a total mess. The twenty or so players that remained lined up and shook the hands of the opposing team. Coach V then told the team to go to the sideline so they could speak. He was beyond pissed off. How could they do that? How could they walk off the field in the middle of the game? How selfish. How inconsiderate. How ignorant.

"Look, I am not going to sugarcoat it. That was an embarrassment. Screw the score, screw that we lost. What happened out there cannot happen on a field. Ever."

All the eyes were on him. Glued to him and his every word.

"I cannot -- will not -- accept that behavior. I don't know about you guys, but when we break down and say family, I mean that. I don't fake it."

There were some nods among the team.

"That selfish behavior will not be tolerated, and it will never be tolerated." He took a pause and a deep breath. It was difficult what to say next because he honestly never imagined something like this would ever happen.

"I am going to make this short and simple. I am going to be there at the practice field on Monday, whoever wants to put the work in and get better and make a run at this thing let's go for it. If you want to quit and leave, go ahead, but I am going to be there on Monday."

A couple more nods with some more eyes looking directly at him.

"Now if you want to be a part of this family bring it in and say it like you mean it."

"Family on 3, 1...2... 3... Family!" The entire team said it with an intensity that shook Coach deep inside.

His entire body was shaking and his arms felt numb. What the hell was he going to do now?

Coach and his wife had an appointment the next day. The baby was the size of an eggplant. The doctor tried to get a look at the baby, but there was too much movement and a clear picture could not be established. It looked more like a bunch of blurs on a screen instead of anything human.

"I am sorry about that," she said as she removed her gloves and shut down the machine.

"Sometimes we can't get clear images, but the heartbeat sounds normal and everything seems good."

They both nodded in approval, but slightly disappointed.

"The good news is I can tell you what you are going to be having. Would you like to know?"

Coach and Rachel exchanged a glance.

"We go back and forth about that," Rachel said.

"But, I think we want to wait for now."

The doctor smile and nodded.

"Totally understandable, you want me to leave you the information in case you change your mind?"

She held up a white envelope and shook it slightly back and forth.

Rachel and Coach exchanged a glance as if to say, what do you think?

"Sure why not," Rachel said.

The doctor smiled and left the envelope on the counter before leaving and shaking their hands.

"So, what are you going to do about the boys who left?" Rachel asked.

"I don't know. I am meeting with the head of the middle school program tomorrow. Hopefully, he can give me some guidance."

Coach was beginning to think this was too much. It was only one game and he already lost two players. Without them, the team was going to struggle. Hell, they might not win another game, but if he let them back, then he looked like a total pushover. It was a real bind.

"Hey, it will be okay. I am proud of you. I love you." She put her hand on his. He smiled as they drove home.

The meeting with the athletic director was at 9 AM sharp. He was only a couple years older than Coach V. He had a buzz cut, a lean body, and pale white skin. Coach V was expecting an older stocky guy but was surprised to see such a young kid running this whole program. He was one of the coaches for the high school team in the city. A team that was always very competitive and routinely winning or in the championship.

"Thanks for coming in coach." He said, extending his hand.

"It's a pleasure Ralph,"

They sat in his office which had equipment and papers scattered throughout. Plaques hung above of former football players and the schools they committed to. Uconn, Yale, Syracuse, and some state schools as well. He also noticed volleyballs, soccer balls, baseballs, and all other equipment throughout. This guy ran all sorts of sports programs, not just football. He also coached high school and worked as a Phys. Ed teacher. "Damn, this guy must be busy as hell. Why am I complaining?"

"Look, I am going to cut to the chase. What happened on Saturday was awful. To be honest I have never seen anything like it."

Coach just nodded and let him continue.

"How do you want to handle the situation?"

Coach was somewhat stunned by the question. He had little experience, especially for such a bold situation.

"To be honest I don't know. I told the kids they were done after the game and part of me wants to stand by that but the other part of me.."

His words just stopped by themselves. He wasn't sure how to say that he needed them on the team for them to have any chance to win.

"Yeah, I understand." he said as he cleared his throat.

"My concern is that going forward football could be a real productive part of these kids' lives. Maybe we don't want to have them walk away just yet."

That was probably the most politically correct way to say what he was thinking. He was impressed by the words of this guy.

"What might be best is we type up a letter explaining the situation and get it out to the parents. Just explaining what happened."

Coach had not even thought of that. After all, there were only a handful of parents at the game. It would be good to keep them informed.

"Also, if you'd like, I have a guy who is willing to help. He coached pop warner and a bunch of other youth football teams over the years. He is a really good guy and is eager to help."

Coach's eyes beamed with excitement. He had been desperate for help, even just another pair of eyes, but an experienced coach sounded like music to his ears.

"Oh wow, that would be great. Thanks! I could surely use the help."

Ralph smiled ear to ear and stood up extending his hand.

"Not a problem at all. I will let him know to come by the field Monday and you guys can get started. Anything else you need?"

"No, thank you again, seriously this is a huge help."

Coach stood up, shook his hand, and turned the corner to leave. He thought about bringing up the pregnancy, but his wife was only three months and it wouldn't have any real impact on the season. He got in his car and drove off feeling much better.

Monday's practice was unlike anything he had seen before. Coach Ben arrived in a white tank top, black shorts, long socks, and work boots. He was about average height but had muscles bulging in his biceps, chest, back, and legs. He looked like he got stung by a bee. He was older, maybe in his late fifties or early sixties, but he in phenomenal shape.

"Nice to meet you, I'm Coach V."

"Coach Ben." he said in a deep raspy voice. The voice you would think of a natural tough guy.

"I really appreciate you coming aboard. We could really use the help."

He nodded approvingly.

"I am going to get them started on stretches. You ready to get started?"

"Sure. Let's do it."

Coach V got them lined up and took two of the eighth-grade linemen as captains. The kids scrambled across the field and spread out as they were ready to begin their stretches.

"Actually, if you don't mind, I got a good idea for warm ups. Could I..?"

Coach V extended his hands. "Please be my guest."

Without a moment hesitation Coach Ben hollered for the team to all line up on the white line.

"No walking! You never walk on this field ever!" It was like he got shot with adrenalin The soft smoker voice transformed into a megaphone.

"I am going to give you a number, 1, 2, 3, 4. You line up at your spot when I give you your number. No walking, no talking, nothing but focus. Understood?"

A couple kids replied with a weak "yes coach."

"I said, is that understood?"

"Yes, Coach!" as the entire team replied in unison.

The structure of practice was unlike Coach had ever seen. The kids responded to it well. There was little to no talking, fooling around, or playing. They were all seemingly focused. A couple linemen played around and coach made them do 10 pushups on the spot. If a kid took off his helmet he ran a lap. Coach V was amazed by how seemingly easy, yet effective this was. He took as many mental notes as he could.

While practice was really structured, the team simply didn't have much to work with. Coach V was hoping that Lito and Terrell would be at practice to apologize and beg to come back. That was not the case. They did the best they could. Freddy was put at quarterback and Vinny moved to running back. They executed basic dives, tosses, and even a play where Vinny threw the ball, but it was clear they needed help. After all, the ball couldn't go to Vinny on every play.

At the very end of practice, Lito and Terrell showed up. They walked casually to the edge of the field and stood there and didn't say a word.

"Coach, it's Lito and Terrell." one of the players said, pointing to them.

"I know, don't worry about that right now. Listen, what I am giving you is a very important letter. This letter introduces Coach Ben who will be working with us for a while. It also explains what happened on Saturday and ensures your parents that it will not happen again. Any questions?"

Freddy raised his hand, "Are they going to come back on the team?"

The whole team looked at both coaches. "That is going to be a coach's decision. There are a lot of things that have to happen before we get there."

A couple of players sucked their teeth with clear disdain.

"Let's focus on our game this Saturday, and remember to get those papers home. Family on three.."

They broke the huddle and Coach V and Coach Ben approached Terrell and Lito.

They had their arms folded across their chests and their heads down.

"What's going on gentlemen?" Coach V asked.

"Not much." Terrell managed to say after a pause.

"This is Coach Ben. He is going to be helping us out this year."

Coach offered his hand and the boys shook it.

Coach was not exactly sure how to start this awkward conversation. What tone should he use? What should he say? It all was unclear.

"How do you feel about what happened Saturday?" Coach asked.

There was another pause.

"Bad." Lito managed to say. Both their heads were down.

"Why?"

Coach Ben interrupted. "You know I heard about what happened and I gotta say I have never before in my 25 years coaching seen anything like that. If it were up to me you guys would never play again."

"Look we don't gotta come back," Lito said

"I am not sure with this attitude you are ready yet. What you did was selfish and inexcusable."

"Guys listen, I…"

"Look we came back to ask if we're back on the team, but we ain't gonna beg or nothing." Lito said, clearly getting a little frustrated.

"No one is asking you to beg, but we do need you to know this is serious. That cannot happen again." Coach V stated trying to calm down the situation.

They both nodded.

"Here's a letter that I need to go home to your parents. It introduces Coach B and explains what happened."

They both took the letter and scanned it quickly. There was a slight pause as Lito looked up.

"Does this mean we can play Saturday?"

"There needs to be a consequence. We gotta talk about it."

Lito shook his head. "Nah fam. We playing or not?"

"I can tell you with attitude, hell no." Coach Ben responded.

Lito laughed and nudged Terrell.

"Okay, good luck without us then." Lito ripped up the paper in front of them and left it at their feet. Terrell crumpled it up and left it on the ground. They turned and walked away without saying another word.

Chapter 8
Game 2

It was time for their second game of the season and it wasn't so much a question of if they were going to win or lose, but how embarrassing it would be. Without Lito or Terrell they would struggle to win even one game, but this week they played the two-time defending champions. Their coach played college football for Uconn. He had darker skin, a stocky frame, and jet-black hair that he slicked back. He talked fast and walked with a visible swagger that accompanied his every footstep. The coaches did the best they could to prepare. They worked on blocking, tackling, they even tried to have Freddy throw the ball with more confidence. He looked slightly better but was still a nervous wreck. They had one trick play where Vinny would get the ball and throw it instead of run. It was going to be used in emergencies.

Having Coach Ben did help with organization and structure. The team was focused on the sideline and it was easier to manage. That was about the only good thing though. Coach saw the size and athleticism of Barrett, the two-time defending champs and he knew they were in for trouble. They had a stout group of linemen, fast athletic running backs, and a quarterback with a solid arm.

The game started off better than he could have expected. On the opening series, the quarterback threw an ill-advised pass right into the hands of Vinny. After that though, it was all downhill. They tried to get the ball to Vinny, but he was hammered every time. Outside, inside, tosses, blasts, they knew where the ball was going and everyone piled on the pour kid.

Defense wasn't much better. The coach figured out he didn't need to throw the ball and just ran it every time. In three plays they were in the end zone and they made a habit of that in the first half. They scored three times and it didn't really seem like they were trying.

With two minutes left in the half coach called the trick play where Vinny throws the ball. Vinny took the handoff and dodged a defender before throwing a decent high pass to the receiver. He caught it and ran five yards short of the goal line before getting tackled.

Their coach was livid on the sideline. He was screaming at the safety to get back and be in position. Coach clapped his hands and padded his guys on the helmet. The kids got excited and celebrated by high fiving and jumping up and down. The play worked, even though they were down three touchdowns.

The second half was a total beat down. They called a passing play to start the half and their quarterback threw a perfect pass right into the hands of the receiver. It was textbook and their side erupted in cheers. The Barrett coach jumped up and down and high fived his kids one by one on the sideline.

His side couldn't be any quieter. What made matters worse was they literally could not move the ball at all. Runs to the left, right, passes, tosses, anything it didn't matter. Coach was powerless to stop anything they could do.

Barrett took out one or two of their starters but left their running back, receiver, and many linemen in the game. As a result, they poured on three more touchdowns before the game ended.

"Kind of seems like they are pouring it on don't ya think?"

Coach Ben nodded but didn't say a word.

Coach ran to the middle of the field and shook the coach's hand.

"Good game coach, good luck with the rest of your season."

He nodded and smiled a wide cocky smile. "You too."

Coach V gathered his team together and told them they fought hard.

"That was a really good team we faced today. Probably the best we'll face all year. You guys gave it your all. You got nothing to be ashamed of."

They nodded, but with heads hanging near the ground.

"Coach Ben, anything to add?"

He shook his head. "No, I am good."

They broke it down and got on the bus. Many of the kids seemingly cheered up as they were laughing and fooling around, talking about how close they were on certain plays, or almost made the tackle. Some even talked about how the other team was cheating by pulling on their jerseys or stomping their feet.

Only two players didn't say a word the whole ride. Vinny and Freddy. They looked out the window quietly the whole way home.

When the bus got back the field, many of the kids left right away. Freddy was the last one off the bus and hung his head as he made his way slowly down the steps.

He was about to walk away, when Coach V grabbed his arm.

"You played hard today. You got nothing to be ashamed of."

Freddy nodded slightly. "Thanks Coach." he put his headphones in and walked away.

"Thanks again for your help today, coach."

"No problem. It was a struggle, but we got through it."

They shook hands.

"I'll see ya Monday. Have a good weekend."

Coach Ben nodded and got in his car and drove off and would never return again.

Chapter 9
Solo

Coach Ben was nowhere to be found on Monday. Coach V thought maybe he got sick, had something going on, but when he didn't show up on Tuesday or Wednesday he knew something was going on. He tried to call him no answer. Left voicemails, and text messages with no response. Hell, he even went on Facebook and found him. He was active, making posts and commenting on political ideas, so he was still alive, which was a good thing, but for whatever reason, he was not responding to Coach V.

Coach eventually got the hint on Thursday and stopped reaching out to Coach Ben.

This practice was torture. Coach tried to install the same level of discipline and organization, but it was both tough on his own and tough when he didn't have the same look, sound, or all-around fear factor that Coach Ben did.

Many players were constantly dancing when they should be lining up in their stance. They threw the ball around on the side instead of focusing on the plays, they threw grass and dirt at each other, they screamed high pitched screams and ran around the field playing tag. All except Vinny and Freddy.

Finally, Coach V had enough. Coach started off Thursday's practice explaining they had a game and they needed to be ready. The team seemed focused and listening, and he thought that maybe he got through to them.

Then near the end at the end of practice while they were reviewing special teams a couple kids were throwing the ball. Coach told them repeatedly not to do it, but he decided to just let it go. He was tired and practice was almost over anyway. Freddy made a great play running down the field finding the ball and making a superb tackle.

"Excellent job Freddy! Way to get in there!" despite the play many of the players ran past Freddy to where the kids were throwing the ball. They were on top of each other wrestling for position.

Coach blew the whistle and pulled the kids off each other.

"What the hell is going on!"

"He threw the ball and it hit me in my junk."

"It was an accident."

"You did that on purpose."

This sounded more like a preschool fight than middle school one.

"Just wait, I am going to mess you up after practice."

"You know what, everyone bring it in." Coach hammered his whistle as players slowly walked to the huddle.

"I said, bring it in!" and he hammered his whistle one more time.

Players rarely heard Coach yell and they quickly sprinted to the huddle.

"Why are we here?" Coach began, with fire in his eyes. His hands at his sides.

"To play football..." one of the players said after a long silence.

"The hell we are. We got people throwing the ball around. Hitting each other in the dick, and running around like we are in second grade."

There were a couple laughs amongst the team.

"See, we think this is funny, but what's not funny is getting your ass kicked."

"I'm here trying to get you to be better football players and many of you just don't care. So why am I here?"

There was silence. No one was willing to tackle that question.

"Listen, I want to tell you something, I am not getting paid a million dollars to do this. I am doing this for you. I am doing this because I believe in this sport, that it can build character, that it can help you be something. This is not play-time; it is not mess around time. I take this very seriously."

Still silence as many heads were looking down.

Coach was getting red and shaking. He spoke not quite in a yell, but in a very stern clear voice that hurt his throat when he spoke.

"I got a pregnant wife at home, a full-time job, and a life of my own. I really don't need this."

Coach rubbed the outside of his mouth with the inside of his hand.

"If you want to be a part of this family, you want to work to get better, you want to play football the right way, then come to practice tomorrow and get ready for our game. If not, please don't come back. Do us a favor and stay home."

He took a pause and a deep breath.

"I'll see you tomorrow. Get changed."

He turned his back and walked away.

While he was waiting for one of the kids to get picked up he got a message from one of his friends from college Bryan.

"Meet up for a drink tonight?"

Thursdays were the days to get wild back in the day, but not so much anymore. Back in college New Haven was deemed thirsty Thursdays. Girls wore skanky dresses, guys were tight Ed Hardy shirts, and it was a drunken blur. Now his idea of a night out was a couple beers and a good slice of pizza.

"Sure, I got one kid, I am waiting on to get picked up, then I can meet up with ya."

"Sounds good."

New Haven has some of the best pizza in the country and Coach V was excited to enjoy some on this brisk Thursday night. Big Daddy's was a small hole in the wall spot a couple blocks from State University where they both went to school. They never used to check for Id's which was a reason they went there in the first place. They would load up on cheap pitchers of beer and pizza before Thursday's then walk downtown to the sketchy clubs in the area.

Coach V parked and immediately saw Bryan in the corner, a spot they usually frequented even back in the college years.

"What's going on bud?" They exchanged a handshake hug greeting.

Bryan was an all-state football player back in high school. He was slightly shorter than Coach V, but he was built like a truck. He had big broad shoulders and thick, tree trunk legs. He could have probably played at a DIII school somewhere but decided to just enjoy college instead.

"Not much man. Been busy with coaching and school, but I can't complain. How about you?"

Bryan shrugged his shoulders. "Same stuff different day man. So glad you could meet up. Come on, let's get a drink. What do you want?"

They ordered pitchers of Bud Light and a large pizza between them. In the college days, it used to be a large each, but even in their late twenties, they had to be conscious of their weight. Too many carbs blew them up like balloons.

"We had some good times here man," Brian said as he shook his head side to side.

"Remember when you challenged that Asian broad to a drinking contest?"

Coach V laughed and hung his head. It was not the first time that story got brought up along with many others.

"You took your shirt off and stood on the bar. It was hilarious. Who won that contest by the way?"

"She was cheating."

They shared a laugh as they ate pizza and drank beer.

"You blacked out on your birthday and threw up all over that table over there. Remember that?"

He vaguely did. There were a couple times he threw up in the bar. He was shocked they still let him in the place. He definitely made his mark.

"Listen, I got some news and I wanted to tell you in person."

Bryan wiped his mouth and stared right at him.

"Oh boy, here we go. You turning gay on me? What is it?"

"Well, I don't know how to say this, so I guess I'll just say it. Rachel is pregnant."

Bryan practically spit up his entire beer. He got up and hugged him with all his might. The kid definitely was strong as an ox.

"Are you kidding me! That's fantastic! Hey, you two are going to kill it as parents. Wow!"

Coach V felt good to see that reaction. He had a feeling Bryan was still living the college life, going out and getting wasted on the weekends and working a mundane 9-5 sales job during the week. They were close but were definitely drifting. Bryan was still single and had no intention of slowing down, and here he was getting ready to be a father. Quite the contrast.

"Excuse me, a round of shots for us please?" He shouted to the bartender who was across the side of the restaurant. It wasn't a big place, but it was a loud enough request to be unruly.

"I don't know Byran, I got work tomorrow…"

He put up his hand not giving his excuse the time of day. "Listen, we're having a shot. You are going to be a dad, wow!"

He smiled and didn't bother fighting it. The bartender poured two tall shots of Jack.

"Congrats my friend. I am very happy for you!"

They chugged the shots down like they used to. It burned all the way down, but deep down the burn felt good.

"Hey listen, what do you say we hit the town tonight. Thirsty Thursday like the good old days. Come on. It'll be fun."

That's where Coach V drew the line. He didn't want to work hungover and he knew where a night where Bryan would lead.

"I appreciate it man, but I really got to get back. Rachel is probably upset already."

"Come on bro, this is a big moment. One bar, Let's hit up Bodega. When you want to go, you can go. If you need to crash at my spot, you can. It's all good. What do you say?"

Coach V honestly would have preferred to go home and sleep, but he was already out and it had been a while since he had seen Bryan. What the hell he could spend another hour in New Haven and then head back.

"Okay, screw it. I'm in."

"Yes! Let's do another round of those shots. Going to be a helluva night kid."

Bodega ironically had not changed since college. Girls in tight dresses, guys in tight shirts in most cases, and music blaring in eardrums like you would not believe. The drinks were cheap, which was nice. It was only $2 bud lights which was unreal. Shots were only $5. Bryan navigated the bar with ease, gliding past the tightly confined dance floor and pushing elbows to get to the front of the bar.

They took another round of shots at the bar and this time he could barely feel the burn.

Coach nodded.

Bryan grabbed one of the girls as they walked by.

"Jessica?"

Her eyes lit up at the sight of him.

"Oh my god, you guys are here? I can't believe it!"

"Yeah, we were getting food and wanted to hit the downtown scene for a while. How's it going? How's school?"

"School is good, busy, but good."

Jessica was the younger sister of a good friend we went to school with. Bryan had a slight fling with her sister, but nothing serious. She was more of a friend than anything.

"What's going on with you two?"

"This guy right here is going to be a daddy!" Bryan said pointing at my direction.

Jessica gave me a big hug and congratulated me.

"You want to do a shot for the big guy over here."

Jessica nodded. "Sure! Let's do it."

They made their way to the front of the bar and took another shot of jack. Coach V made his way to the bathroom to pee. Luckily, there wasn't much of a line, but the place reeked of piss and vomit, just like it had many years ago. *Some things never change.* When he came back, he scanned the area for Bryan, but couldn't find him. Not by the bar, not where they were before until he saw him on the dance floor with Jessica. He was grabbing her waist and she was grinding up on him. Not too aggressive, but it was not exactly PG either.

Coach V slowly backed away and headed out of the club. It was a long walk to his car, but the breeze felt good.

All of a sudden, Coach was in his bed. He had a splitting headache and he was totally changed. He didn't remember a thing. How did he get home? What happened.

He rolled over and saw Rachel sitting up rubbing her eyes.

There was a long pause. He knew instantly that he messed up. He was wasted last night, way more drunk than he thought, and prayed he didn't do anything bad. Worst of all he drove home.

The silence seemed to last forever. Until she finally spoke.

"You, don't remember anything about last night do you?"

Coach shook his head. It hurt to breathe. He saw tears slowing going down her cheeks.

"You were wasted. You passed out on the kitchen floor. I had to carry you upstairs."

That was bad. He felt awful, irresponsible, and immature.

"I am really sorry."

She shook her head.

"I can't do this. I am pregnant and I can't keep doing this with you. You need to figure this out."

This had happened before. He had blacked out and pissed the bed, or dropped his phone in a pool, or passed out somewhere without the ability to wake up until morning. It didn't happen every time he drank, but it happened way more than it should. Although one time is probably more than enough.

"I know. I am sorry. I am going to work on changing. I promise."

Rachel shook her head again, sternly, not with rage, but seemingly utter disappointment.

"I have heard that before, and it is very different now. You need to do it for our family. You need to figure this out because I can't keep doing this. I won't do this."

Tears poured out of her eyes like gushers after those words. Those words were like knives through his heart because they were so true.

He rubbed her leg softly. He felt so low.

"I am sorry. That is not fair to you."

She nodded. "Nope. No it isn't"

She dried her eyes and wiped her face. There was a pause as they both stared in opposite directions. He didn't know what to say and she didn't either.

"I have to get ready. You should shower."

They spent the rest of the morning getting ready in silence.

School was torture. Coach was hungover, tired, and just wanted the day to end. Practice was going to be miserable. He debated canceling it, but with a game tomorrow he knew he couldn't.

"You look tired," a couple of the kids told him. Man, he must really look like garbage if they were noticing.

"Yeah, not much sleep last night."

The day dragged by but he got through it. He took his time changing and getting ready for practice. He knew it was going to suck. The kids were seemingly content on losing and acting like idiots, and his headache and lack of energy weren't helping matters.

He took the slow drive to the field and parked in his usual spot. He got his bag together and slowly got out of the car with his head down. Then he felt a slight tap on his shoulder. He turned around. It was Lito with his head down and hands in his pockets.

Chapter 10
Lito

It was a blisteringly cold morning as the wind smacked Lito in the face. He skimmed over to the bedroom window in a half-awake—half-asleep state. The window didn't close fully, which was nice in the summertime, but in the fall and winter, it was cold as hell. He had to walk carefully as his two younger brothers were at his feet. It was like a dance to get to the window without waking them, and if he woke them with his feet the crying would never stop, and his mom would not be happy.

Lito made his way to the bathroom, sprayed some deodorant, and quickly brushed his teeth. He put on the same hoodie he wore a couple days in a row, but it smelled clean enough, so it seemed fine. Then, when he was finally ready, he woke up his two younger brothers to get them to school. He shook them by the shoulder forcefully to make sure they were jarred awake. He learned that you needed to do it with a pretty careful amount of force. Too soft and they would just roll over and go back to bed. Too hard and they could roll off the mattress and create a whole scene.

He made them each a bowl of cheerios.

"Cheerios? Again?" they complained.

"Shut up and eat it. And eat it quick. We're running late."

If the boys got another tardy the truancy office would call and he would have to hear about it. His mom was already in a pissy mood when she came home from work, but if she had to deal with that situation. It would get real ugly.

The boys ate reasonably quickly and they walked briskly to their school. Luckily they both went to the same elementary school and it was on the way to his middle school. The wind was unreasonably strong. Normally the walk was not too bad, but today it was windy and it shook them side to side as they made their way.

"Alright, go inside. I'll see you guys after school. Be here right on time. No messing around. Don't be late!"

He gave them a playful hit on the shoulder and watched them go into school.

Then Lito turned around and headed back the other direction to his house.

He met up with his friend Manny. Manny was a sophomore in high school, he was tall, skinny and smooth. Lito admired his Jordans, chains, and swagger, even though he would never tell him that.

"How's it going, youngblood?" Manny asked as they exchanged a handshake

"Not bad, bro. Just another day you feel me?"

"I hear that. It is cold as hell today. Gonna freeze our asses out there."

Lito shrugged his shoulders. It was what it was. Small price to pay for the job, and it sure beat the hell out of school.

Lito and Manny grabbed a juice from the corner store and then made their way down the block to the spot. It was on the corner of Howard and Jerome. It wasn't too busy a neighborhood, but it wasn't too quiet either. The store in the near distance was a nice reason for hanging around the corner.

They sat on the corner and drank their juice and tried to stay warm. Routinely putting their hands in their pockets.

"How's the team? You guys looking alright?" Manny asked.

Lito took a sip of his juice.

"I quit. Coach is buggin'. Those dudes are straight ass."

Manny raised his eyebrows.

"Damn. That sucks. Coach Bryant usually holds it down."

"Nah, it's not him. It's this new white coach."

Manny shook his head.

"Yeah, that's the problem. Coach Bryant gets it in man. We had a squad."

A car pulled up alongside them and parked. The boys waited a moment and then looked at each other.

"I get this one. You got the next one. Cool?"

Lito nodded.

Manny slowly approached the car. Lito scanned the surroundings. He had been out here a week now, but he still got nervous.

Manny shook hands with the driver and walked back confidently.

"Not a bad start to the day."

Manny secretly showed Lito the cash in his jacket pocket. He saw at least two $20 bills folded up messily.

Lito nodded and continued to scan the area.

"You straight?" Manny asked as he nudged Lito in the stomach with his hands still in his pockets.

Lito nodded.

"Listen, don't worry about that white dude. You straight? Now you can make some serious money out here with me. When word gets out about you, things will only get better. Trust me."

It was hard to disagree. Manny used to be beyond broke. Wearing torn up sneakers from Walmart, or stupid off-brand T-shirts. Now he was rocking Jordans and serious chains. It was hard not to be impressed.

The waiting was the worst part, but the weather got a little warmer, and the wind settled down, which helped. Still, Lito hated waiting. They would go in the store to get a juice or a pop tart every now and then, but sometimes it was an hour of just sitting, which could drive you insane. He sometimes played on his phone, stalked Instagram or YouTube, and Manny was easy to talk to, but still, it got boring.

Another car pulled up and stopped for a minute. No one got out so Lito slowly made his way over. His heart was racing as he slowly approached. It was a Honda Civic. Slightly rusted by the wheels a light gray color and dirty as hell.

"What's good?" Lito managed to say with as much courage he could muster.

Confidence is what Manny told him. Remember to be confident. You are in charge.

"You good, youngblood?" It was a man maybe in his late twenties or early thirties. He had a buzz cut and sunglasses. Rap music played lowly in the background.

"Ten or Twelve o'clock, my watch broke."

"Ten," the man said without missing a beat.

"Lito reached into his pocket and pulled out a small bag. He remembered to keep it tight in his hands. No air, no one can see. He clenched his fist tight like he was holding a football and bracing for a big hit.

"Alright. Thanks."

Lito carefully leaned over and braced for a high five handshake. He felt the paper connect with his hand as he let the bag go at the same time. It was perfect like the quarterback handing the ball off to the running back. He put it in his pocket and examined it carefully.

He nodded, and the car slowly drove off.

He slowly made his way back to Manny with his heart beating out of his chest.

"You're getting pretty good at this."

Lito nodded and took a deep breath. He may be getting better, but he was beyond nervous every time. Maybe that wore off over time, but he didn't know. What if that guy had a gun and held him up? What if it was an undercover cop? Those questions swirled around in his head each time he stepped up to do his job.

"Yo, can you do me a solid and grab me a juice? I gotta take this call."

Lito nodded and walked into the store to look for the cheap juices. They were only 99 cents and grabbed one for Manny and himself. He was happy the day was almost over. Just another hour and they could get out of here.

Lito walked out of the store when he froze. There Manny was with a cop right in front of him. He slowly made his way back into the store. *Damn.* This was bad. He didn't know what to do. Does he run? That makes it obvious and maybe the cop goes after him? Or calls back up? Does he go up to Manny? No, that's an even worse idea. He gets totally screwed. His breathing got heavy as he weighed all the options in his head. He put one of the juices in the trash as it was totally unopened. The owner looked at him funny and shook his head. Then he slowly walked out the door not even making eye contact at Manny. He turned the opposite way and headed down the block. He walked quickly, but as inconspicuous as possible. Not stopping, Not looking back. His hands in his pockets, his head down as he just kept walking. He kept walking until it was a dead end. He then sat on the curb, put his head down, and cried with his head in his hands.

Chapter 11
Practice Before Game 3

Coach V had a lot on his mind that Friday. He was hungover and had an upset, pregnant wife to deal with at home. He had a headache that felt like death and he had a game tomorrow that they would most certainly lose.

So when he felt the tap of Lito on his shoulder, he almost said "Not this. Not today."

But then he saw the look in Lito's eyes. It was a different look than normal. Lito usually had a look of confidence, arrogance might be a better word. His head up high, smile ear to ear, and a hitch in his walk that indicated that it was a treasure just to be around him.

This time though Lito seemed much different. His eyes were set on the ground. There was no smile, and he moved his feet side to side nervously.

"What's going on Lito? We got a game tomorrow. I don't have much time."

There was a pause as Lito continued to shuffle.

"I want back on the team."

Coach took a deep breath. Part of him was happy, the team needed him, but he hated this confrontation. He knew he had to be tough and firm. You can't just walk off the field in the middle of a game and expect to come back. He also knew some of the kids were going to be salty seeing him come back and they were right to be.

"Listen, what you did was unacceptable. I have never seen anything like that. You let me and everyone else down."

Lito had his head down and nodded.

"What do you have to say?"

Lito took a second. "I was mad."

Coach was stunned. "Yeah, what else."

"I ain't gonna do it again."

That was a start. He could tell this wasn't Lito's specialty. He wasn't used to apologizing or having to ask for things.

"I can tell you are sorry, but what happened was ridiculous. I don't have time to deal with people walking off the field. Is that what you're going to do when things get hard? Just quit? Walk away?"

He shook his head.

There was a pause as Coach took a deep breath. He never dealt with anything like this before. There was no "how to punish a player" chapter in the handbook. He thought about having to punish his kid in the future. That would surely be an adventure. He also thought about the guts it took to come back and ask for forgiveness. To own up to a mistake, when it would be ten times easier just to walk away and say forget it.

"Listen, there are certain things you gotta do to make this right. You are not just going to be put right back like nothing happened."

Lito nodded. "I'll do what I gotta do."

That was a lot different than the kid who tore up the paper and left it at his feet not too long ago. The exact response Coach was hoping for, but never thought he would get.

"You are going to start running today and you ain't going to stop until I say so."

Lito nodded. He put his stuff down and took off his shirt and then started running around the field. Many of the players had looks of shock. He knew he was going to have to address this issue, but he wasn't sure how. "We are going to suck without him" was not appropriate no matter how true it was true.

He tried to completely ignore the fact that Lito was running around their practice, but that was not possible.

"Coach, is Lito back?" Freddy asked right away.

"We'll see, right now I need us to focus. We got a game tomorrow."

Practice was much sharper than normal. Probably because Lito was there and everyone was a little more on edge and looking to impress. Freddy's handoffs and tosses were on point, and Vinny did a decent job hitting the hole, but the blocking was poor. Vinny had little to no help on the outside and when he tried to turn the corner he was greeted by multiple defenders. They needed more talent. Plain and simple.

Coach rubbed his hand on his face in frustration and did something he knew would cause a lot of controversy.

"Lito, get in here."

Lito quickly sprinted over to Coach. Breathing heavily with sweat all over his bare chest.

"Go in at halfback we are going to run 28 Toss with Vinny. I want you to block for him."

He nodded and ran to the huddle. A couple players sucked their teeth. Coach ignored them. They broke the huddle. Freddy took the snap and threw a near perfect toss to Vinny. Vinny broke the line and followed Lito. Lito leveled one defender in front of him and got all the way to safety securing him out of the way so Vinny could go all the way to the end zone. It was perfect.

Coach then called the same play with Lito getting the ball. A couple players rolled their eyes, but as soon as Lito took the toss he was greeted in the backfield by two defenders. He spun out of a tackle, juked the other defender and broke to the outside. Either the line missed their blocks, or purposely let the defenders go by. Regardless, Lito got to the edge easily and followed a great block by Vinny to go all the way to the end zone. Very few 13-year olds could make a run that impressive. Heck, very few high schoolers or kids in college could move like that.

Practice ended and Coach got the team together.

"Today, was a good practice. We were focused and got some good stuff done. I'm very happy."

Some players nodded, some looked toward the ground, and a couple had eye contact right with him.

"Some of you asked me about Lito. I have made the decision that what happened was a big mistake. He learned from it, and we all learned from it. Lito, you got something you want to say?"

Lito stood up and faced the team. He rubbed the back of his head uncomfortably and shuffled side to side while he spoke.

"I'm sorry, for what I did…"

He stopped.

"And…?"

Freddy and a couple others said egging him to keep going.

"What else…?"

"It won't happen again? I don't know. I'm not good at this…"

"Okay, okay. That is good. It is not an easy thing to do. Actions are going to speak louder than words. Remember we stick together. This is a family. Let's be ready to battle tomorrow, no matter what."

"Let's break it down. Family on 3."

They broke the huddle and many players scattered all over. Coach grabbed Lito.

"You had a great practice today. I am proud of you."

He nodded his head. "Thanks."

He walked off into the distance. As Coach got in his car and drove home. Fearing the conversation with his wife.

Chapter 12
Rachel

Love. That is all he wanted. He desperately wanted to hold her close to his chest, to feel her breath against his neck. To rub his hands slowly up and down her spine. For her to caress the back of his head and rub it side to side.

Now, when he put his hand on her leg he could feel her uneasiness. It was subtle, so slight that if you didn't know Rachel you wouldn't think twice, but he knew. It was real.

He knew it was selfish. She was pregnant, tired, and frustrated. She was going through something he could never know, never understand, but he couldn't help it. The distance between them was growing, but the worst part was he loved her just as much as he ever had. She was gorgeous, her hair bright and blonde, her body trim but voluptuous. Her smile glowed as her eyes twinkled like light green crystals. They used to be all over each other. Their kisses filled with passion as their lips and tongues moved in magical unison. Cheeks and noses rubbing against each other with a gentle tenderness. It was only a couple months ago but it felt like ages.

Now there were no kisses goodbye. No hand holding, no twinkling of the eyes. There was nothing. It was dark and empty.

"I am going to meet up with the guys for a drink. It's Byran's birthday, and I said I would stop by for a bit. I shouldn't be too long."

He thought about staying home, and maybe that would have been the better, smarter move, but he felt like he needed to get out. It was uncomfortable and maybe blowing off some steam would help things a bit. Plus Byran was one of his best friends since elementary school. He had to at least show face.

She nodded. "Okay, have fun."

He leaned in for a kiss on her cheek. It was cold and hard. He backed away slowly. She had an uncomfortable, uneasy look on her face as he slowly backed away, got in his car, and drove off.

He got to the bar up the road. It was a small townie bar, filled with middle-aged men, an older couple or two. He ordered a jack and club soda and sat in the corner. He wondered if it would always be like this. Would she never love him ever again? Was he doomed to a life without intimacy?

"You want to start a tab?"

He totally forgot where he was as he looked up to see the bartender with his hands on his hips.

"Yeah," he nodded and ruffled through his wallet to hand him his credit card. Then he noticed the black and white picture that fell out. It looked like one of those psychiatric tests doctors give the people who might be insane.

He examined the photo the paper was smooth and soft. It was hard to believe in that photo was his future child. He kept trying to picture him or her, but he couldn't. He closed his eyes and couldn't imagine. He threw back the drink and it burned on the way down. He ordered another one, and another after that one, keeping his eyes on the photo after each sip.

He got in his car and started to drive off. He knew he drank too much because his vision was way blurrier than normal, but thought he could make it the mile down the road without an accident. Despite some wild turns, he did make it into his driveway. Instantly, he got sick and threw up outside his car. He then stumbled in the front door after struggling for a minute to find the right key to enter. He looked in the fridge for something to eat, but couldn't find anything good. He checked the freezer and saw some frozen meatballs. He unpacked them and put them in the micro-wave. While he waited, he put his head down on the counter.

The next thing he knew he woke up in the middle of his kitchen floor face down. His pants were soaked and his head was pounding. He slowly rose up and made his way to the bedroom. His wife was fast asleep in the bed. He quietly grabbed a pair of clean underwear, and slowly took off the dirty pair. He then slowly turned around and headed to the living room trying as hard as he could to be as quiet as pos-sible. He laid down on the couch with a blanket and pillow and tried his hardest to close his eyes and sleep.

Chapter 13
Game 3

Coach woke up with a dry mouth and a pounding headache. He was already running a bit late to get to the field. He quickly showered and changed. He did so quietly as to not disturb his wife. She was fast asleep. After his shower, his wife was sitting up in bed. She was on her phone with an expressionless look on her face.

"Hi," he said.

"Hi…" she said back.

He quickly got his black polo and pants on. He wasn't sure if she knew about his incident last night. He hoped to god not, but she obviously knew he wasn't in the bed with her. He was not sure what to say or how to approach the subject, so he didn't.

"How are you feeling?" he asked.

"Okay." was all she said. Her eyes still on her phone.

"When's your game today?"

"Noon."

"I might try and come if I feel up to it."

He nodded. "Okay, no pressure."

He walked over toward her.

"I gotta run to meet the team. I love you."

He reached over and gave her a kiss on the forehead. It felt cold and uncomfortable.

"Good luck," she said as he walked out the door, got in his car, and made his way to the field.

The team they were playing, Fairleigh had not won a game this year, just like them. Their coach dressed in baggy jeans and a ripped-up shirt and work boots. His son was the starting quarterback and was by far their best player, but the rest of their team was small and unorganized. Kids were tossing the ball around and hitting each other during warmups. They had one other tall slender kid who the quarterback was throwing to. He ran good routes and caught the ball effectively. That was something they definitely had to watch.

The biggest question was should he play Lito? It was only one practice, but to lose 3 games in a row would be brutal. Without Lito, they would struggle to beat anyone. He thought over the options but then brought over Freddy and Vinny.

"Guys, I am thinking of playing Lito. He can really help us and he seems changed. Before I do, I wanted your thoughts. You guys are the captains. What you think?"

They both looked at him and shrugged.

"It is up to you, Coach. Do what you want." Freddy said.

Vinny agreed. "Up to you, Coach."

That didn't make things easy. He was hoping for a more definitive answer, but it was clear that they were not in love with the idea of bringing him back.

"Okay guys, go get ready. Kickoff will be soon."

Coach thought about it some more and then got the team together in a huddle for a talk.

"Listen, this is a very important game in our season. We need to win this game in order for us to keep our season alive. Coach took a deep breath and then made eye contact with Lito.

"Lito, I am going to have you play today. I've seen a change in you. I am going to take a chance. I hope to God I'm right."

He nodded. He saw a couple players with their heads down but chose to ignore them.

"I need you to stay on number 88, he's tall and can catch, but you are faster than him. Lock him down."

He nodded. "Yes, Coach."

"Vinny, I am going to have you watch the quarterback, wherever he goes, you go."

"Yes Coach, he said."

"Listen, we are the better team. Let's get out there and show it."

They broke it down and got to their sideline.

Fairleigh got the ball first. On the first play, the quarterback dropped back. Sure enough, he looked right toward 88, but Lito had perfect coverage. The quarterback tried to laser the ball in there, but Lito got his hand in there and the popped up in the air and hung up there almost in slow motion before it ended up landing in the hands of Freddy. Freddy used both hands to grab it and corral it in his stomach, then he was tackled instantly.

The sideline erupted. On their very first play on offense, Coach called a toss play with Vinny with Lito lead blocking. It was a perfect toss by Freddy, Vinny took the handoff and made his way to the outside. He followed a perfect block by Lito and ran all the way to the end zone untouched.

Fairleigh's offense was a cluster mess. They had countless false starts, holding penalties, and timeouts. The other issue was they threw the ball way more than they ran it. Coach didn't know much, but he realized quickly that passing in this league was tough. You didn't have the time. The quarterback had to run for his life half the time and he struggled to do anything productive, only gaining two first downs in the entire first half.

The cougar offense was starting to struggle a bit as well. The Fairleigh coach loaded up the box to stop the run, making it very difficult to run with almost the entire team at the line of scrimmage. It didn't help that he had to run it to Vinny almost every play. He didn't want to give Lito the ball yet, and he couldn't pass, but the Fairleigh coach was starting to catch on. He needed to mix it up.

"Okay, we are going to go fake 28 quarterback keep. Remember this play, Freddy?"

He nodded.

"Just remember to protect the ball and follow Lito's block. No one should be near you."

The defense was all stacked at the line. They screamed, "Watch 15!" Vinny's number.

Freddy took the snap and faked the toss to the right, and then rolled out to the left. Nearly the entire team followed him. Freddy had nothing but green grass and one defender to beat. Luckily Lito was there and delivered a perfect block knocking the defender to the ground. Freddy ran in for his first touchdown of the season.

They were up 16-0 in the first half.

Things were looking great. Coach was so impressed with Lito and his selfless ability to deliver fantastic blocks. Blocking was not something anyone really liked to do, but it is essential for any play to work. He wanted to let Lito know he appreciated him and his change; he decided to give him the ball.

"I am going to give you the ball, Lito. You have been blocking your ass off. I am proud of you. We don't score without your blocks on either of those plays. Which side you want?"

He smiled. "Left."

"Okay, let's get it, fellas."

Sure enough, the toss to Lito was right at his chest. He took it perfectly and ran to the outside. Surprisingly, the defense had an idea it was coming because there were four defenders there. Seeing this, Lito cut back to the inside. The entire team had to switch directions. They tried to catch up to chase him but they couldn't. There was only one defender within reach, Lito stuck out his arm to deliver a vicious stiff arm that threw back the defender as he fell to the ground. Touchdown. 22-0.

They ended up winning the game by that score. They shook hands and made their way to the opposite end zone so cCoach could speak to them.

"You should be proud of yourselves today gentlemen," he said with a clenched fist shaking in front of him.

"We showed heart, we played well, and we played together. Everyone contributed. Everyone helped make this win possible."

He clapped his hands and patted a couple of his players on the shoulder pads.

"But this is just the beginning. Let's get ready Monday to put the work in and make a run at this."

Many of the players nodded their heads convincingly. He meant what he said. He was proud of them and they all did play well. It felt good.

"Let's break it down, family on three."

They broke it down and scattered back to their sideline to grab their stuff. Coach could see in the near distance a slender teenager shirtless on his bike with the sun at his back. It was difficult for him to recognize the figure with the sun in his eyes and as he was about to walk over the kid quickly turned his bike around and rode off in the distance.

It was Terrell.

Chapter 14
Terrell

Terrell always thought back to five years ago. He closes his eyes and can picture the brisk fall air, the leaves a mix of browns, yellows, and oranges. More so he tries to hang on to the feeling he had that day of going to his first football game with his dad.

He hadn't seen his father in a couple weeks. He was always working. He worked early in the morning, and then his second job in the evening, along with every other Saturday. It wouldn't be strange for Terrell to go a month without seeing his dad. He did call him every night though. He asked him how school was and how everything was going. His mom begged him to keep the conversations short, which was frustrating, but he loved those conversations.

His dad came bright and early like he promised. He arrived in his souped-up pickup truck, with tinted windows and crystal-clear silver rims.

"How we doin' little man?" His father gave him a big hug and lifted him in the air. He was well stronger than he looked. He was slender but had modest muscles that popped out of his t-shirts.

"You excited? We're gonna see the G-men live! Your first football game!"

Terrell nodded his head emphatically. His dad came over sometimes on Sundays and they would watch the game. Sometimes they would go to Rudy's a dark lit restaurant that smelled like smoke and dirt. Many of the people there always looked mean and were covered in tattoos. They smelled bad and swore all the time.

But today was going to be different. A real live football game. He had his Tiki Barber jersey on and his Giants gloves for if it got cold. His mom insisted.

"Be careful you two." His mom said as they stood on the porch.

"Of course, we are gonna have a great time." he rubbed his head playfully.

"Just remember what we talked about okay?"

His dad took a deep breath. "Why you always gotta be like this? Why can't you just let me take my son to a football game?"

"I am just trying to protect our son! Someone's gotta do that!" Her voice was getting louder. Not quite a scream, but definitely louder than normal.

"Yeah, yeah, give it a rest already would ya? Come on, T," he said as he put his hand around his son and they walked to his car.

They drove off with Biggie Smalls blaring in the speakers and smiles glued to their faces. Terrell tightens his eyelids trying to hold onto that feeling. The wind caressing his hand leaning out of the passenger side window, the bass of the rap song barreling out the speakers, and his father sitting right by his side for one final time before he was gone forever.

Chapter 15
Comeback

Coach wasn't surprised when Terrell showed up to practice on Monday. He was on the same bicycle that he was on for the game. He was shirtless and he was the first one there.

Coach didn't want to admit it, but they needed him. Without him they were decent; they would beat up on average or below-average teams, but soon enough word would get out that all they did was run the ball and any coach that had half a brain would stack the box and mess them up. It was primarily a running league, but you needed to pass the ball a little to be effective and keep the defense honest.

Terrell gave them their best shot to be successful.

"What's up Terrell?" He asked as Terrell instantly got off his bike and approached him. He wiped the sweat from his face before he spoke.

"I... I was wondering... if I could rejoin the team Coach?"

Coach knew that was what he was going to ask, it was just a matter of how he was going to ask it. He really wasn't in the mood to go through an entire speech, but he knew he had to. He explained how he let the team down, and let himself down. He was a little easier on Terrell for some reason. Probably because Terrell was a bit more soft-spoken than Lito. He was easier to coach and talk to. He was very surprised a kid like this would quit ever.

"I know Coach. What I did was wrong. I am sorry."

Coach nodded. He extended his hand for an old-fashioned handshake. Coach shook it and padded him on the head.

"You got some running to do before you get back out there."

He nodded and smiled as they walked on the field together.

The hardest part of the practice was breaking the news to Freddy. He wanted to approach him first, but unfortunately, Lito got to him before he got the chance.

"T is back y'all. This is about to be lit!"

You might as well have hit Freddy with a hammer. He looked so defeated.

Coach wiped his hand over his face to try and wipe off the feeling of guilt. He called Freddy over. Freddy came over with his head down and his eyes wide open.

"Look, Freddy, I still haven't made a final decision on who is playing quarterback." that part was a lie. Terrell was a far superior athlete and thrower, but it sounded good and he owed it to Freddy to sugar coat it a bit.

"You are a major part of this team. Without you, we are not successful. We need you."

Freddy nodded his head but didn't say a word.

"You understand?"

He nodded again.

"You okay?"

"Yeah," he finally spoke.

"Okay, let's get ready and have a good practice."

It might have been their best practice all season. Terrell seemed to be the missing piece they needed. Coach started off with Freddy at quarterback and had him run a couple running plays. They went fine, but then he called some basic passing plays to Vinny, and that is when Freddy looked like a mess. The ball came out like a wounded duck as it fluttered through the air unattractively time after time. Coach told him to keep his elbow up, bend his knees, and twerk his body to get some momentum behind the throw. None of it made a difference. Freddy's throws just came out unattractive and uncatchable. The only good thing was the pass was so bad even a defender couldn't catch it.

"Coach, put T, in at QB." Lito told him.

Coach put up his hand.

"One more time Freddy, try and relax."

Freddy did the play again and the ball again fluttered at Vinny's feet. Coach had no choice. It was getting embarrassing now. He felt bad, but there was nothing he could do.

"Okay, let's change this play up, Freddy you go to tight end on that side and T you go in at QB."

T nodded.

"Remember you got Vinny on the deep fly, Lito on the quick out, and Freddy on a slant. Your first option is Vinny for the big play if he is open."

Terrell nodded. "Got it."

On his first try, T stepped back in his three step drop and unleashed a near perfect pass that spiraled in the air beautifully. Vinny was well past the defender and the ball landed in his hands as he outran the entire defense. The whole team erupted.

They reviewed some of their basic running plays and defense and then broke it down.

Coach made a point to go to Freddy one last time.

"I meant what I said Freddy. We need you on this team. Keep your head up, okay?"

He nodded.

"If anyone gives you trouble let me know. I'll handle it."

He nodded again with his wide-eyed look still glued to his face.

"Thanks Coach."

Freddy walked away slowly as Coach got in his car and drove home.

Coach got home and his wife had dinner ready. She was always cooking even pregnant, which he tried not to take for granted.

"Thank you so much for dinner. Sorry I am late. Long day and I had to wait for a couple kids to get picked up. How are you feeling?"

"I am good, just tired. I might lie down."

"Oh, okay. You want me to get you anything?"

"No, I am okay, just tired."

"Okay, I'll join you in a bit."

"Okay, goodnight."

"Goodnight."

She slowly walked past him and made her way to the bedroom as Coach ate the chicken parm in the dead quiet on the kitchen table.

Gameday came and it was a big one. They were playing Welsh, the team they lost to in their first game of the season. The game where both Lito and Terrell walked off the field in the fourth quarter. Coach knew it was going to be a test. They needed to stay focused, avoid the trash talk, and stick together. Forget winning, he just hoped they could all walk off the field without fighting or anyone quitting.

"Not everything might go our way..." he explained.

"But it is important we do not stop battling. We stick together and keep working hard. You understand?"

"Yes, Coach!"

"They might say some stuff to you and you might want to respond, but do not. Play your game and let your pads do the talking."

"Let me say this again. We are in this together. We are a family. No matter what happens."

He tried to look at the whole team, but it was nearly impossible not to glance at Lito and Terrell and make sure they caught his message loud and clear. They stared right at him, which he took as a sign they understood loud and clear.

They broke it down and got ready for the game.

Coach had a very simple game plan for defense. Stop their QB from running around. That killed them last game. He put Vinny at one outside backer spot, and Lito at the other, and Terrell at safety.

"Watch their QB he is going to run. We just need to stay in front of him and tackle and we will be fine. Do not let him get to the outside."

Coach motioned his hands to try and illustrate the point.

"If we keep him contained in the inside, the game is ours, if we let him out, we are going to be watching him run into the end zone all day."

They nodded.

Sure enough on first down the QB tried to take off right and he was greeted by Lito who made a fantastic tackle. On second down, he tried left and Vinny was there to wrap up and bring him down. On third down, he tried to throw the ball, but Terrell read it, stepped in front of the pass, and nearly had an interception. It was fourth down and they had to punt.

It was the Cougars ball. Coach usually called running plays to start the game. They were safe and it got some of the nerves out, but the Welsh defense must have known that. The first three plays got modest gains of only one or two yards on handoffs to Lito, which put them in 4th down and five.

"Screw it lets air this out," he told his guys.

And sure enough, he called the pass they had practiced all week. Terrell dropped back and had defenders closing in, but he had just enough time to get off the deep pass before they brought him to the ground. The defense was still not expecting a pass and Vinny easily out ran the defender, who might as well have been a mile away from him. The ball landed perfectly into his arms as Vinny carefully brought it to his chest and then jogged into the end zone comfortably for a touchdown.

Terrell came over to the sideline and Coach patted him on the helmet.

"Hell of a throw."

Terrell had a smile ear to ear.

With the threat of the pass, the defense was all mixed up. Coach's whole play chart was working. Lito scored on a toss to the right where he outran two defenders to dive in the end zone. Vinny scored on a reverse where the defense bit on a fake to Lito, but it was really Vinny who had the ball and ran down the opposite sideline for a touchdown. Terrell scored on a fake toss, quarterback keep, where he juked a linebacker out of his shoes and effortlessly made it to the end zone.

When it was all said and done, the final score was 35-0. The Cougars were all smiles, high fiving each other and slapping their shoulder pads.

"Be proud of how you played today," Coach said.

"You guys executed perfectly. This is what we are capable of."

He saw many players nodding along.

"If we stay focused, we got a real shot at making a run at this thing."

"What do you say?"

The team cheered loudly.

"What's that I can't hear you?"

They cheered even louder.

"Championship on 3!"

They shouted as loud as he ever heard. As they broke the huddle and headed toward the bus he had a smile ear to ear. All the practices and long days seemed worth it for this feeling when things came together and the team was successful. There was a deep feeling of accomplishment that they were a part of something special. That feeling numbed his whole body until he got in his car and got ready to go home.

Chapter 16
Terrell Part II

Terrell's dad just had to get some gas before the game. He switched from the music to the radio, which was blaring the pregame show for the Giants. Terrell turned up the volume a bit to hear some of the chatter about what the experts thought.

"You want anything from inside?"

"I'm good. Thanks."

Terrell heard one of the commentators talking about how the Giants had no shot to win. That made him angry. How could he say that? No shot? He wanted to punch that guy. You always have a shot. That is what his dad told him.

A loud argument got his attention Terrell saw his dad arguing with a light-skinned man about the same age. He couldn't make out the conversation, but they were screaming at each other and the man was pointing his finger in his chest.

Terrell didn't know what to do. Part of him wanted to run out and help his dad, the other part said that was an awful idea. So he froze. He just stayed in the car and watched.

His dad shoved the man, and the guy fell back hard on the ground.

The guy got up and reached behind his back and pulled out a gun. Terrell had never seen one before.

At that point, Terrell bolted out of the car.

"No!" he shouted, which got the man's attention.

His father tackled the guy and started pounding him in the face hard. His fists made an awful thud each time they connected with the man's skull. It was hard to tell if the noise came from the fists, or the back of the man's head colliding with the pavement, or maybe a combination of both. Terrell's father quickly picked up the gun, pointed it at the man, who raised his arms, desperately trying to grab the weapon, but they were shaking uncontrollably, and could not stabilize. There was a loud bang. His father dropped the gun at his feet. He was breathing heavily, there was blood on his hands and sweat covering his whole body.

Terrell looked at the man. His eyes were open and blood covered his entire face.

"Come on. We have to go."

Terrell didn't argue, he didn't speak, he didn't even think. He simply got in his dad's truck as they drove off.

Chapter 17
Home

When Coach got home, he felt really good about himself and the team. This feeling after a win, when everything went right, it was something that he had back in his wrestling career. He did not win often, in fact, he lost far more than he won, but he caught fire later in his high school career and made a nice run in the conference championship. He thought about when he caught his opponent and was able to stick him for a pin. That feeling was total euphoria. The ref raises your hand as your opponent slouches in defeat. This was different though. He was the puppet master calling the plays, organizing the troops. His designs led to scores, which led to points, which led to celebrations. His pep talks led to confidence, which led to victories. Sure, the players had to execute, but he had to put them in the right spots to succeed.

He opened the door and his wife was making dinner. It was meatballs and pasta. Her meatballs were incredible. They were a mix of pork, beef, and chicken and the sauce was the perfect texture. Not too soupy, but not too thick either.

"How'd it go?" she asked as she stirred the pot.

"We won; the kids played well."

"Congrats," she said, as she never took her eyes off the big pot. Her response was with little emphasis or enthusiasm. Cold and distant.

"Thanks," he said as he leaned in for a kiss. She slightly moved her cheek offering it to him. It was what many do for in-laws they don't like or maybe a perverted uncle.

Dinner was ready and they ate and talked about the nursery.

"Maybe you can help set up the crib tomorrow?" she asked.

"Sure, no problem."

There was an awkward pause. He wanted to bring up the issues, say he was sorry again, talk to her about it, but it was uncomfortable, and the moment didn't seem right, so he didn't.

"Do we need anything else for her?"

"Umm, well we have to see what we get from the registry. Once all those gifts come in, we will know what we need."

He nodded, as they finished their dinner in silence.

Coach picked up the plates and started cleaning the dishes. He never minded doing that and thought it was the least he could do if his wife was going to cook dinner.

"Thank you for dinner. It was really good." he leaned in for another kiss and it was again greeted with her cheek. This time a little less awkward, but that might be because he was prepared and expecting it.

"You're welcome."

She was tidying some blankets and pillows in the living room while he finished up cleaning.

"Listen, I am pretty tired, I think I am going to lie down, downstairs."

He was not expecting that. It had become a ritual to watch a movie or some shows before bed. In bed, she took up nearly three-fourths of the bed with her giant pregnancy pillow. He didn't mind obviously as he wanted to make sure she was as comfortable as possible.

"Okay, are you sure?"

"Yeah, I am sure."

She stepped closer to him. "Good night," she gave him a kiss on the mouth. It was a closed kiss -cold, sharp, and quick.

"I love you," she said as she slowly backed away.

"I love you too," he replied.

She then went downstairs and closed the door as Coach sat on the couch and turned on the TV flipping through the channels for something to watch.

Chapter 18
The Streak

Success was becoming routine for the team. They won their next three games. It was starting to become fun. Things always became easier when you were winning and this was no exception. They won each game by multiple scores with a combination of Terrell running and throwing, the dual threat of Vinny and Lito running and catching passes, and a defense that was aggressive and tackling well. They went from a last place team to being tied for 1st with Barrett, the only undefeated team in the league. The defending champions for three years in a row.

The first time they played it was a massacre, but they also didn't have Lito or Terrell. Still, this was the best team in the league and Coach knew they had to play their best to have a chance.

Coach V felt good about his team, but this was the real test. If they could beat Barrett, then maybe, just maybe, they could have a shot at the championship. Hell, if they could make it a close game that would be enough to put everyone on notice. This is a team that hadn't lost in two years, and they definitely acted like it.

During warmups, the Barrett coach came over and shook V's hand. He was a former athlete and packed on a couple pounds post college. Still, he was in decent shape with jet black hair and a visible swagger that accompanied his movements. Everything he did seemed to have a little extra juice to it. The way he chomped his gum loudly between his back molars, the way he smiled in a slightly crooked way, with his head cocked to the side. It was hard to identify, but Coach V felt it every time he was around him, and it bugged him like a fly that just won't stay away from your food.

"Good luck today, Coach," he was chomping on his gum with great intensity as he stuck out his hand. Coach shook it with careful force.

"You guys had a good game last week. Looking pretty good."

Coach nodded and looked at his team. I guess word had gotten out that they were not a pushover anymore. With the return of Terrell and Lito, they were definitely something, and he was not surprised to see the Barrett coach had figured it out.

"Yeah, we had a couple good games. It should be fun today. I gotta get my guys ready. Good luck again coach."

They shook hands one more time and the Barrett coach even threw in a light pat on the shoulder as they went their separate directions. He wasn't a bad guy by any means, hell, he even sort of liked him, but he also didn't forget about passing plays when they were up by thirty. He didn't forget about how awful it felt to have his kids hang their heads while he chomped his gum and smiled that crooked smile. He didn't forget about how he left some starters in so his team could keep their shut out. He would love to return the favor today.

There was no big speech or pep talk. Coach V got his guys together and just told them to play hard and play aggressive.

" Let's give it to these guys. They are not ready for you." They broke the huddle and got ready to get the ball.

On the very first drive, things went better than good. Terrell gave a toss to Lito who was met by three defenders. It looked doomed, but he kept his feet moving and the tackling by Barrett was uncharacteristically poor. He broke three tackles, fought his way to the outside, and spun his way into the end zone. The Cougar sideline erupted. It was a tremendous effort play by Lito and it showed just how tough a runner he was. You could not ask for a better way to start the game. Coach V was jumping up and down, so excited that they got out to an early lead before he finally calmed down and realized how he had to keep it together. It was only the first quarter after all. There was a long way to go.

On the following kickoff, the Barrett runner tried to juke to the right but kept the ball in his left hand. Terrell, wisely, yanked his arm where the ball was and punched it out. Freddy happened to be right there and dove on the fumble to give the ball back to the Cougars.

Coach V called a fake toss to Lito and a naked quarterback bootleg. Terrell faked the toss perfectly to the left and rolled out to the right with nothing but green grass. Practically the entire defense bit on the fake and Terrell could have walked into the end zone. It was 14-0 before you could blink.

Barrett got the ball back and responded right away. Their quarterback dropped back and threw a wobbly pass, but the receiver had the presence of mind to go back to the ball high in the air and make a beautiful catch. It was a textbook two hand grab where he caught the ball at its highest point. Vinny played it well, but not well enough. The receiver snatched the ball out of the air as Vinny fell to the ground. The Barrett receiver then turned around and ran all the way into the end zone.

Fortunately for the Cougars, that was all the scoring Barrett would do for the rest of the game. Coach V responded with the same fake toss play, but instead of Terrell running, he hit Vinny for a beautiful pass. The defender was in an impossible spot when Terrell rolled out. He had to choose between Vinny and Terrell. Would he rush at the quarterback? Or would he stay with Vinny? Either way, he was doomed, and when he finally rushed at Terrell, the ball sailed softly over his head and perfectly into Vinny's hands for a touchdown.

The Barrett coach responded by trying to pass the ball much more, to catch up, but their defense was ready. The quarterback dropped back and tried to fit the ball into double coverage when it was picked off by Lito. Lito ran the ball to the five-yard line before he was tackled. They scored on the next play with a handoff to Lito. The quarterback dropped back again but took too long to get rid of the ball. Freddy came at the perfect time and hit the quarterback from behind. The ball squirted on the ground before Terrell picked it up and ran it all the way into the end zone for a touchdown.

When it was all over, they had won 42-7. It was Barrett's first loss in two years. The last play consisted of Terrell simply taking a knee, something Barrett never did when they played the first time, or maybe ever, for that matter. There was some pushing and shoving after the game. Coach V could not make out what exactly was said, but he wanted to stop it immediately.

"Let the scoreboard do the talking! Don't say anything! Let the scoreboard do the talking!"

Luckily, the players separated and listened to him, which was not always a guarantee. The last thing he wanted was anyone to get in a fight and get suspended.

The Barrett quarterback took off his helmet and slammed it on the ground. He did not enter the handshake line after the game as he sat on the bench with his head in his hands.

"I want you to say two words, and two words only. Good Game. You got me?"

A couple players responded with "Yes, Coach." but many did not.

"You got me?"

"Yes, Coach!" was the resounding response, which seemed like the majority if not all of the players.

They shook hands and fist bumps and luckily there were no incidents. Many of the Barrett players had their heads down, and some were even crying. When the coaches met, V extended his hand. The Barrett coach shook it quickly and simply said, "good game." He then rushed past Coach V with tremendous speed. Coach V knew he didn't like losing and that little gesture of rapidly shaking his hand, felt like a crappy thing to do. Coach always shook hands even after the tough losses, or the best wins. He was fired up now, and wanted to let the kids know it.

The team gathered together like they always do, and they had smiles from ear to ear. Coach was planning on telling them to stay focused, not to get too carried away, but his heart was racing, and he started talking before he could even really think.

"Today, you guys did something no one has done in two years. You beat that team's ass."

They applauded and hooted and hollered. Coach waited a moment and then got louder and more aggressive.

"You guys played with heart and intensity and you didn't quit."

more claps and cheers, but Coach was screaming now. Very loudly over them.

"You see they aren't used to losing. They don't like that, but we have been there and done that. Now we are the ones handing out he beatdowns. We are the ones who are going to mess people up."

He was turning red; he could feel heat engulfing his entire body. He stuck his pointer finger and put it to the sky.

"Right now, we are the best team in the league. And no one, and I mean no one, is going to stop us."

All the players looked shocked. Mouths open. Faces expressionless as coach spoke. They never saw him this full of passion.

"Get in here and break this down for me!"

The kids all shouted and raced into a huddle.

"Championship on three, as loud as you can. I want those dudes over there to hear you!"

"1...2....3..."

"Championship!"

They shouted and broke the huddle. Some jumped in the air. Some patted each other on the back or exchanged handshakes, but all of them were smiling. Coach peeked over at the Barrett huddle. Their coach was gesturing to his right and his left, demonstrating different stances, positions, and other mannerisms. Coach V nodded his head and smiled as he got his bag and walked his way toward the bus smiling right along with the rest of the Cougars.

Chapter 19
The Talk

In the grand scheme of things, it was not that big of a deal. There were much more important things in the world than a middle school football team. Coach V had to remind himself of that even though he knew that. Still, on his way back home, he caught himself time to time drifting off and reliving a Terrell pass or a Lito run. He cocked his head to the side and smiled at that feeling of jubilation. Then he would quickly and literally shake his head to snap out of that moment. Three weeks ago this team looked hopeless. They were without a quarterback and running back. They couldn't tackle and could barely even gain a yard. Now they had a real shot at winning it all. Wild.

Coach pulled into his driveway. His wife was in the kitchen cooking beef stew. Her stew is fantastic. Soft, not too chewy, and juicy. One of his favorite meals.

"How'd the game go?"

She was wearing an apron and her hair was pulled back. She still looked beautiful. Eight months pregnant and all. Her belly was out now, but not to a ridiculous degree. It was like a small basketball was in her shirt.

"We won," Coach said as he leaned in for a hug and a kiss on the cheek.

She accepted the kiss and hug, offering her cheek without protest.

Coach washed his hands and cleaned his face.

"Oh, come here. Come here quick."

Coach quickly shook his hands in the sink and pivoted to his wife. Her tone did not indicate danger, but it indicated speed and he tried to be as quick as possible.

"Feel." she took his hand and placed it on her stomach. Placed was not really the right word. She kind of yanked it on there. She put his hand low on her belly. Very, very low. It was awkward until he felt it. It was a little flutter. It felt like a small ball that rolled against her stomach.

He hadn't thought about it much directly. Being a father, being responsible for another human being— it didn't seem real yet. Coach was so busy with work and coaching and the rest of life he really didn't have time to think about it that much. That little flutter though. That slight kick or bounce of an unknown body part; that made things a bit clearer. There was a baby on the way and things were going to be so different. He took a deep breath and let it out slowly.

"Crazy right?" she said as her eyes lit up as she asked the question. I guess his expression revealed how surreal it was to feel his future child alive inside her.

"Unbelievable," he managed to say. Still in shock.

"So, this came in," She held up a small white envelope with no markings or distinguishing figures.

"I know we talked about waiting, but…" she took a long pause as she shook the envelope slightly from side to side. She was smiling now, and he was relieved to see that. He knew things had been rough between them and that was a lot of his own doing. He knew he had some work to do, but he was glad to see that she was cheerful and happy.

"I don't know if I can wait?" she managed to finish.

Coach V agreed. He told Rachel that he was okay waiting, but that was a lie. He also told her that he would be happy with a son or daughter. That too was a bit of a lie. He wanted a son more than anything. A little boy to play sports with. To take fishing, even though he hated fishing. A girl would be fine, but a son, that would be perfect.

"Okay, let's do it."

They sat down on the couch and each took deep breaths. They would have laughed about how in sync they were if they both weren't so nervous.

"You have to do it. I can't," she said as she handed him the envelope.

Coach V accepted. He carefully tore open the back. Being sure to take his time and not rip anything. He then took out a small piece of paper that was folded in half. He unfolded the paper which had a small ultrasound of an alien-like creature, which was indeed their future child. On the paper, there was a clipart picture of a baby and above it in large black letters it read "CONGRATULATIONS ITS A GIRL."

They both took a minute to survey the paper.

"Wow. A girl," Coach said the words in almost a shock.

"Yes a girl," Rachel said as she picked up the paper and examined it further.

They sat back on the couch for a moment. Coach V put his arm around her and she placed her hand on his leg. They were quiet for a moment as they stared ahead looking at nothing in particular.

"Can I be honest?" she asked.

"Sure."

"I know this is a bit of a surprise. I know we both were kind of secretly hoping it was a boy."

"Wait, I didn't know you wanted a boy?"

She nodded. He smiled and laughed. She mentioned having a boy a couple times, but she always played a bit more of "whatever we get I am fine with as long as he or she is healthy." Maybe the way she started with "he" was a giveaway or the way she always talked about some boys' names more than girls. The clues were starting to come together well after the fact.

"But, I think this is a blessing. And I think it is okay for us to be a little disappointed."

Coach nodded.

There was another pause. He was thinking about his mom— She would have loved a little girl. He was not one of those people who truly believed in heaven or hell. He was not super religious or really into the supernatural, but at that moment, he did have a feeling he couldn't describe. Logic indicated it was purely chance. They had a fifty-fifty shot at a boy or girl, but he liked to believe that it was something more than that. That this was something like fate.

"What are you thinking about? How do you feel?" Rachel must have noticed him trailing off for longer than normal.

"I… I'm thinking about my mom." saying that gave him pause, and Rachel put her hand on his back.

"It might sound weird, but maybe this is her way of speaking to us. Maybe this is her doing…" He was communicating it very poorly.

She nodded her head. She didn't really say anything, but they had talked about his mom a lot. Rachel had both her parents, but she had a way of listening to him that others didn't. She was supportive, understanding, and most of all compassionate.

He turned his head to look at her and she looked back at him.

"I love you," he said.

"I love you," she responded.

He leaned in for a kiss. It was not sexual. Their mouths were closed with a sliver of space in between, but their lips connected with a great amount of force. Careful, not reckless, but filled with compassion and emotion. It felt good.

They ate dinner together and talked about baby names. Coach drank two glasses of wine as they ate their stew and laughed about what their daughter might look like.

When dinner was over, Coach washed the dishes and thanked Rachel. They usually would watch a movie, but tonight they just talked.

"Now we just have to think of a name," he said.

"I know it's a lot of pressure. Any ideas?"

Coach shrugged. "Nothing yet, but it will come."

They hugged again in the middle of the living room. They kissed again, as they embraced the new member of their family. They were not just a couple. They were finally a family.

"I think I am going to go to bed," Rachel said.

"Okay, I am pretty tired too."

Rachel had a puzzled look on her face that was hard to explain.

"I think I am going to sleep downstairs again tonight."

"Are you sure?"

She paused for a moment but then nodded.

"Yeah, I just need to be alone. I hope you understand."

Coach did not know what to say or how to respond. The best he could do was nod right back ever so slightly.

"Okay, if you think that is best."

She leaned in and gave him a hug and the same kiss they shared earlier. This time it felt much different.

"Goodnight. I love you," she said as she looked him in the eyes.

"I love you too."

She then turned around and walked downstairs.

Chapter 20
Coach V: Mama's Boy

Most days come and then go just as quickly. But then there are those that drag on forever. Days that hold an unbearable weight that no matter how hard you try you can never carry. Today was one of those days. He took a breath letting the cold days deep air sting his insides. The rain was not coming down violently but steady and sad. My father and I walked to the cemetery, our heads down treading across the squishy surface. My father firmly carried a pot of fake flowers under his right arm. They were for my mother who died three years ago. We wanted to give her real flowers, she deserved them but, for whatever reason, they were forbidden by the cemetery. Something about maintenance or landscaping, but most likely it had to do with laziness. The pot contained all the bright colors my mom loved. The pinks, reds, yellows, and blues, but her favorite color wasn't in there. White. I remembered when I was younger I asked her why. It's so dull, boring, and lifeless. She just laughed smiled, tilted her head to the side the way she always did and said,

"Well white may look plan on the outside, but on the inside, there is so much more."

"What do you mean?"

"White contains all the colors. It allows for your blue eyes and my brown hair. White may look boring on the outside, but on the inside, there is a whole rainbow of colors waiting to come out. And the inside is what really matters."

My father placed the flowers right beside the words "Mother" on her gravestone. It was hard to believe it has been three years since she passed. I was a freshman in high school when it happened now a senior. I put my head down, closed my eyes, and tried to concentrate on her. Her face, her smile, her laugh. I squeezed my eyes harder searching deep for some resemblance of her. Anything.

Hey ma, I hope all is well…hope you can hear me… Tomorrow's the big day. I'm wrestling in the conference championship, but I guess you probably already knew that.

There was a long pause as I waited for something. Anything. I wanted so badly to envision her but all I saw was darkness. All I felt was nothing

I just want to say I miss you and I hope wherever you are you're happy.

I opened my eyes and lifted my head. My father bent down wiping off dirt from the gravestone with his bare hands. After a few long minutes of wiping he rose to his feet. With his hand covered in dirt, he made the sign of the cross. He folded his hands together at his waist head down in silent prayer. I wondered what he was thinking about, I wondered if he had any luck communicating with mom but, I never had the nerve to ask and he never told.

He made another sign of the cross, this time much faster than the first.

" You want to get out of here champ," my father said, draping his arm over my shoulder. They then ended up at Old Towne. It's a small Italian place my father goes once a week after church on Sundays.

"Just two Pete?" Donna asked, picking up two menus.

She was a heavyset middle-aged woman who lost a husband to cancer. She'd always been a family friend, and I was decent friends with her daughter who had the reputation of being pretty crazy. For the past month or so Donna has been around the house a lot more. Never anything too crazy, not like she's moving in or anything, but I'd see her watching T.V. with my dad, preparing dinner, or just alone reading her *Good Housekeeping* Magazines in the Living Room. She's always been nice to me, smiling, asking me how things were going, and I would reciprocate her kindness with that of my own. It was all a formality though. Deep inside her recent and growing presence was becoming hard to ignore, and it started to bother me. I can't pinpoint the exact reason, but it was clear that having Donna around simply didn't feel right, and I didn't know how to bring it up, or if I should at all.

"Anything you guys want to drink while you look at the menus?" Donna asked while my father and I sat down in the soft booth.

"Just water for me," I said flipping through the menu's pages.

"I'll have a bud, dear." My father replied.

Donna nodded and then took off quickly.

"How's school going?" my father asked while turning the pages of the menu himself.

"Not bad. Math's a struggle, but I'm surviving."

School never weighed too heavily on my mind or my fathers. It was always my mother who cracked the whip in that department. I thought about college because that's what every high school kid thinks about. The problem is money is tight and my grades weren't exactly elite. I was hoping wrestling would provide me a scholarship like it had for others but nothing was coming up. My father and I had a college talk a few times. He never said much on the subject. Never told me I couldn't go but, the way he looked down and talked in short abrupt sentences made me think he wasn't in love with the idea either.

"You guys ready to order or do you need a few more minutes?" Donna asked with pen and pad in hand. I must admit for a larger woman she moved pretty quickly.

My father took the initiative.

"The usual for me dear."

Donna nodded then directed her eyes at me.

"Ok, what about you sweetie?"

"Uh, I'm just gonna stick with the water thanks." Donna raised her eyebrows at my response.

"You sure you don't want anything James?"

She was still one of the few people that called me that. I'd be lying if I said it didn't bother me.

"Yeah, I'm sure."

"Come on buddy you gotta get something." My father said playfully hitting my arm. I'm Not sure if he really was concerned about my eating habits or didn't want to eat alone.

"Uh, I don't know I am right on weight, I don't feel like cutting tomorrow morning or later tonight."

"Oh I heard about the championship," she said while patting my arm.

"Congratulations!"

"Thanks, but I haven't won anything yet. Tomorrow is the big day."

I was pretty surprised Donna knew. I tried to keep quiet my personal affairs. I didn't want to be that guy that beat his chest every time he achieved some success. Plus getting to the championship didn't mean a damn thing if I couldn't win it.

"Just get something for dammit you haven't eaten all day." My dad's eyes squinted and he shook his head from side to side; the trademark angry look of Peter Voytek.

I wasn't in the mood to argue and my dad was not in the mood to back down. I figured I would just end this now rather than causing World War three.

"I guess I'll just have a small salad." Donna nodded and collected our menus.

"And if you don't mind put the Italian dressing on the side...please." She smiled nodded and then walked off.

The silence between us was building quite aggressively. My father took a few big sips from his beer and I did the same with my water.

"So, tell me about this championship..." My father asked rubbing his mustache with is pointer finger and thumb.

"What do you want to know?" I asked.

"Do you know who you're going against?" My father asked taking yet another sip from his bottle.

I tried not to think about my opponent. He was the kid who beat me twice already this season. He was a hundred and sixty pounds like me but made of stone. He was getting a scholarship to Penn State and I was lucky to come up with the money or grades to go to college period. He was the number one kid in my weight class since the beginning of the season and I never broke past tenth. It was the same plot you've heard about a million times. The guy who everyone expects to win versus the kid who is just lucky to be there.

"He's this kid from Danbury. He's pretty good, we'll see what happens."

"Just don't get hurt... How's your shoulder?"

I made the mistake of telling my dad I popped my shoulder earlier in the season. Ever since then he's been obsessed about it.

"Knock on wood, it's been good."

That was a lie. Truth is every time I stepped on the mat, I was nervous as hell that my shoulder was going to pop out. I have seen some of the toughest wrestlers in the world lying on their backs in tears when trainers aggressively popped their shoulders back into place. It scared the hell out of me.

"Let's keep it that way. I don't need you in the hospital."

150

Donna came back with the food placing it right in front of us respectively.

"Here you go guys, enjoy." Donna quickly walked away.

" What time is the match tomorrow?" My father asked picking up his fork.

"Hard to say. I probably won't wrestle till around four or five, but it all depends on the other matches."

My father nodded as he placed a fork full of fish into his mouth.

"Maybe I'll come by and watch," he said.

I coughed as some of my water got caught in my windpipe. My father had never seen me wrestle before. He talked about coming here and there but never followed through.

"If you want. You don't have to though, it's really no big deal either way." I said.

My father chewed for a few moments.

"Yeah, I'd be nice to see you wrestle."

I tried not to take his proposal too seriously. There were multiple reasons for his absences. Sometimes it was work. Other times meeting a friend and sometimes no excuse at all. Something just came up I guess.

We finished the rest of our dinner in silence. I couldn't help but eat all of the salad. It had been a while since I had seen a whole plate of food in front of me. I felt a little guilty about it but, figured I could cut weight earlier in the morning if I really needed to. If I was over it wouldn't be by more than half a pound and a jog and some pushups should knock that off.

Donna came out of nowhere gently placing her arm on my dad's shoulder.

"Pete, I hate to bother you, but do you think I could get a ride home. My daughter took the car and I can't seem to get a hold of her."

She was leaning on the table her low-cut shirt allowed my father and I to view her black bra. It was an image that I could have certainly gone without.

"Of course, Donna, not a problem." My father replied.

"Thanks, Peter, don't worry about a tip."

"Don't be silly dear, you're always good to us, the least we can do is return the favor." Donna smiled then backed away red engulfing her face.

"Okay, let me just grab my coat."

The drive home was less than a mile. Donna sat in the front next to my father while I rode in the back. Once we got home Donna and my father kept their seatbelts on.

"Hey, buddy I think we're gonna get a few drinks down the road. I'll see you back in the house a bit later ok?"

I nodded, just happy to finally escape the brief, yet uncomfortable car ride. I craved sleep and just the thought of waking up early tomorrow made me cringe.

"Have a good night, James," Donna said as I quickly opened the car door.

"Good Night, Donna,"

"I'll catch you later buddy," My father said sticking his head out of the car window.

I looked back at them as they slowly pulled out of the driveway and drove off down the road.

When I finally got into bed sleep wouldn't come. I tossed from one side to the other. Flipping the pillow over a few times to feel the fresh cool side. I stared up at the ceiling blinded by the darkness of my bedroom. I turned to my side, closing my eyes desperately hoping for sleep.

My alarm clock blasted me awake at six o'clock on the dot. On sheer will and will alone I managed to roll out of bed and get dressed. I grabbed my singlet, headgear, and wrestling shoes and shoved them into my bag. My head down, I quietly walked out of my room making my way to the bathroom. Just as I was about to open the door, I saw it pull open and Donna's face.

"Oh my, James, you scared me." She placed her hand on her chest. Her hair was all tangled, makeup vanished giving a rather plain look. Never before has Donna stayed a night at our house. At least not when I was there.

"I'm sorry, I was just gonna use the bathroom then catch the bus."

"Oh that's right, today is the big day, huh?" She was fixing her hair looking back in the mirror while she talked.

"How are you getting there dear?" She pulled out a hair tie from her pocket and went to work on her hair.

"Oh, I was just gonna walk. It's only a mile or so up the road," I said.

"Nonsense, James let me take you. I picked up my car last night"

"Oh it's quite alright, I can walk."

"I insist it's on my way, I don't mind at all."

Her eyes were gazing at me now. I shrugged my shoulders.

"Okay, let me just go to the bathroom first," She smiled.

" Take your time, I'll go warm up the car."

The air was thick and cold that morning, but it was nothing compared to Donna's car. I instantly regretted not walking, but it was too late to turn back now.

Luckily the first minute of the ride we sat in silence. It was awkward, but I preferred it to anything sort of conversation.

"My daughter didn't call me till one o'clock last night," she fumbled with the radio as she spoke.

"Not a word about where she'd been or what she'd been doing..." She took a deep breath and let it out with thunderous relief.

"I worry about her James…" Her eyes glanced over at me, and I made the mistake of getting caught in her Medusa-like gaze.

"You know your father is lucky to have you."

I perked up after that comment. I knew where this conversation was going. I didn't want to hear about my father, myself, and what Donna thought about our relationship. I just wanted to get on the bus and figure out how the hell I was gonna win the championship on barely any sleep. My head hurt, my mouth was dry, and all I wanted to do was sleep.

"You never give him any problems. I told him that, told him that last night," She paused.

I didn't want to hear about last night.

"He's so proud of you James. He tells me that all the time—"

"Thanks Donna, it's a left up here."

She carefully turned the wheel with both hands. Another pause as Donna cleared her throat.

"James I know I have said it before but I'm really sorry about your mother."

I clenched my fists while they rested on my thighs.

"We were friends. She was one of a kind. A great person."

My hands were starting to tremble; face beginning to turn a slight shade of red.

"Donna, I would appreciate it if you didn't talk about my mom…"

The car slowed. I could feel her eyes move off the road toward me.

"Come again?"

I used my hand to wipe my mouth before I spoke.

"Just please don't talk about her like you knew her."

Donna lightly placed her right hand on my shoulder.

" James, I know what you're going through, it must be tough—"

I moved my body abruptly to the right forcing her hand off my shoulder.

"No, Donna!. No! you don't know anything about me or what I'm going through. So just stop!, stop it please!"

That was the first time I have ever raised my voice at an adult since fifth grade. A slight feeling of guilt crept inside me. The silence rose in the car for the rest of the ride. The really weird thing is my reaction felt completely out of my hands, maybe because I was tired, maybe because It was hungry, or maybe it was a combination of both, but it was as if I had no control over my words, instead they controlled me. I thought about an apology, Donna was not a bad person. I didn't hate her. Maybe she deserved one, but the words wouldn't come. We sat in silence as we pulled up to the bus.

Donna pulled the car to the side and let me off.

"Good luck, James," her bottom lip was quivering sporadically, moisture in her eyes ready to burst.

"Thanks, and thank you for the ride," as I exited the car the cool breeze struck me in the face. I walked onto the bus with an uneasy feeling I couldn't identify.

Once on the bus I attempted to compensate for the hours of sleep I lost last night. The problem was when I closed my eyes all I could think of was Donna and my dad. *How could he do that? It was all bull. The wiping of the gravestone, the passion, the pictures he saved, the love he claimed to have, it all meant nothing now.* He wasn't hurting like me. He was forgetting her, replacing her.

I sat on the bench looking up at the bleachers unable to see my father. I wondered if he would even show, or if this would be another one of those times where something came up. Another failed promise. Right before my match, my coach pulled me aside. I was expecting some big inspirational speech. Something he probably spent all night writing, perfecting the right words, using the right tone. Something not too emotional but not too subtle either.

"Hey, you had a great season. Give 'em hell out there, alright?"

He supplied his comment with a soft pat on the back. I guess even my coach didn't give me much of a chance to win.

I looked across the mat and saw my opponent jumping up wildly into the air. It was a warmup routine that displayed quite a bit of athleticism not to mention fear into opponents. Finally, the ref clapped his hands and instructed us to come to the center of the mat.

My opponent was about the same height as me but at least twice my size. It was hard to believe we were in the same weight class, but it was not uncommon for wrestlers to drastically cut weight to dominate a lower weight class. This guy would normally weigh fifteen pounds heavier if he didn't drastically cut weight. He was from Danbury, Connecticut. A no nonsense wrestling town. They were so dominant they had to travel out of the state to find competition, going to New York or New Jersey almost every Saturday. Nearly every weight class had someone in Danbury in the finals, and if they didn't it was a huge disappointment.

This kid was one of their captains. His name was Lawton. He had bleached blonde hair that was cut short, which was a tradition that all Danbury wrestlers upheld for the championship. His arms were bulging vein-covered phenomenons. His shoulders stood like two mountains with a face in the middle. His torso was defined as if he were carved out of stone. A body that seemed without weakness. A figure that was not human. I got down into my stance prepared for the worst. Usually, I was nervous before matches but as I bent my knees bracing myself for the biggest match of my life, I was not wired with aggression, nor paralyzed with nerves. For the first time ever, I was completely calm and I had no idea why.

The whistle blew, and he charged at me. We fought for positioning, pushing each other forward and backward, side to side, but moving Lawton was like trying to move a massive boulder. Eventually, his strength got the better of me. Within a minute, he grabbed my legs and turned me in the air with a textbook double leg takedown. I was face down on the mat. Using brute force, my opponent turned me to my side and then to my back. He had all his weight on top of me. Slowly, I could feel my energy escaping, it was hard to breathe, difficult to see, and impossible to escape. He put more and more weight on my chest as he methodically pushed his bodyweight right on my stomach. I thought of how embarrassing it would have been to come this far and get pinned in the first period. I refused to end my wrestling career that way and pushed back with all the force I could muster. I used my neck and legs to bridge and try and keep his pressure off of me and keep my shoulders from hitting the mat. I feared that at any minute the ref could pound his hand on the mat and blow the whistle and it would all be over. Eventually, the whistle blew, and I survived the round down five points, but it felt like a million.

The second period was much like the first. He took me down within the first thirty seconds. Again, he fought like hell to turn me over and pin me, but I continued to fight. I worked hard to build my base rising to my knees, then to my feet, eventually escaping his grasp. I was rewarded one point for my efforts, which was my only point of the match thus far. I tried to create some offense, but Lawton was just as quick as he was strong. He sprawled and avoided all of my takedown attempts. When the whistle blew to end the second period, I was down ten to one. I was near exhaustion. Each breath I took felt like a deep sting inside my ribs. My mouth was dry and my whole body was numb. I felt like a big bowl of jello. I looked over at Lawton. His hands were on his hips, chest pumping in and out. That gave me a sliver of hope that, at the very least, I was tiring him. That he was human. Beatable.

Then came the last period of my wrestling career. It was too late to win by points, so my only chance was to pin him. I tried to search inside myself for something to get me going. I tried to find some sort of inspiration, motivation but there was nothing. My shoulder was starting to feel numb, and it was getting harder to breathe. Part of me considered just giving up. There was no chance. This guy was too fast, too strong, too tough. I got in my stance and the whistle blew to start the final period. This time, he charged at my legs immediately. Once on top, he barreled his elbow into my neck. It was a dirty trick that wasn't exactly legal, but many refs let it go especially in important matches. The pain shot down my neck, taking over my entire body. I closed my eyes and gritted my teeth, fighting to keep my head up and work to my feet. I thought of Donna's giggle. Oh God, how I hated that ear-piercing screech. I worked to my knees. I envisioned her hand around my father's waist; they were laughing together, holding each other close. I rose to my feet, ripping his hands from my grasp. I was now facing him now, looking at an opportunity to attack. I thought about the future; Donna and my father lying together in the living room when I came home from school. Me having to create some friendly b.s. toward her; having to act like I cared at all about anything she had to say.

I dove at his legs, completely catching him off guard. He couldn't regain his balance in time and awkwardly he fell to his back. Hands, arms, bodies, were scrambling for position. It was a test of wills, a jigsaw puzzle of his body and mine. I closed my eyes and saw my mother. She was lying on her hospital bed, fighting for her life as the cancer ate away at her body. Her eyes were closed, but there was the steady beat of the heart monitors. It was just her and I, as I held her hand begging her to fight, begging her to keep going.

My muscles contracted, and with every single cell in my anatomy I grabbed a hold of a leg and what felt like a head and squeezed for dear life.

Beep... Beep....Beep... Then the beeps suddenly stopped. I squeezed harder, hoping, praying for something to happen. Hoping for her eyes to open or for her hand to squeeze back, but there was nothing. Nothing at all. She was gone.

The official's whistle blared, and I opened my eyes. I was on top, in control, yet failed to pin my opponent. I shook his powerful hand and the ref then raised it as the official sign of victory. I ran over to my coach and received the tightest hug I have ever gotten in my entire life.

"You worked your ass off out there. You got nothing to be ashamed of, you hear me?"

I nodded. Disgruntled, yet appreciative of his comments. I was standing in the center of the gym with my hands on my hips, head angled toward the ground. I did everything I could, fought as hard as my body would allow, but it didn't matter. I guess sometimes losing is inevitable no matter how hard you fight.

I felt a hand gently grasp my shoulder.

"Tough loss, buddy," it was my father. The first match, the only match he had ever seen me wrestle.

"You aren't hurt, are you? Shoulder okay?" he rubbed my arm after the question.

"Yeah, it's fine."

"You worked real hard out there. That kid looked pretty tough."

He kept his hand on my shoulder. All I could do was nod my head.

"Come on, buddy, let me take you home, we'll get something to eat on the way. Whatever you want."

I shook my head. I was happy my father came, but there were so many times he wasn't there. Lots of matches that I had won, lots of memories of which he was never apart of.

"I'm going to go back on the bus with coach. I left some of the stuff on there anyway."

"Are you sure?" he said scratching the back of his neck nervously.

"Yeah I'm sure. I'll see ya back at the house."

I turned my back and quickly made my way out of the gymnasium into the cold air.

Throughout the hour ride, my coach told me stories of his championship match. Something about how he lost by one point and how it was the toughest feeling he's ever felt. I didn't say much. I felt bad being so abrupt to my father. My frustrations maybe were too visible. He did after all come to see me wrestle. Maybe I was just being unreasonable. There was another part of me that resented his lack of interest. He told me time and time again wrestling was not his "thing," that he couldn't "get into it." But, if nothing else it meant a lot to me and that should have been enough.

I thanked coach for the story as we got off the bus. He told me I was a pleasure to coach. I thanked him again and began my walk home.

It was very common for wrestling matches to take all day, sometimes lasting eight or even ten hours. It was dark now as the streetlights barely illuminated the sidewalk. I was about half a mile from my house when I looked up at the nighttime sky. The moon was cut perfectly in half. One half white circle looked beautiful; it was pearl white and glowing like a giant marble high above. It was unreal how something like that could be out there, seemingly in reach yet millions of miles away. But then there was that other half of the moon, the half that was covered by darkness. The part that I couldn't see and couldn't see me. I closed my eyes and took in another sting of the cold air. The burn felt good.

By the time I got to my house, it around was 12 o'clock so I suspected my father to be asleep. I quietly walked to the back and unlocked the door making sure I closed it softly. I walked into the living room surprised to see him lying on the couch and not in his bed.

"Hey buddy," my father said.

"Hey," I responded.

His expression didn't change as his eyes stayed glued on the T.V. It was some movie with Clint Eastwood, but not one of his older films when he was shooting bad guys in the Wild, Wild West. This was one of his new ones where he's much older and looks angry all the time.

I took a seat on the sofa right next to my father. His hands were crossed over his head, eyes captivated by the T.V. and only the T.V. Things felt awkward and I wanted so badly to break the uncomfortable silence. I was conjuring up an apology trying to get the words right in my head before I spat them out.

"You know this girl that plays in this movie, she reminds me a lot of your mother."

I looked at her; it was a younger girl probably in her mid to late twenties. She was sleeping in a hospital bed, and she did look a little like mom, but far too young to be that accurate.

"Yeah, I guess a little bit," I said.

The movie looked familiar.

"Dad, haven't you seen this before, I think I saw you watching it the other day?"

He nodded. That was a pretty big understatement. For at least a week straight my dad was watching this movie and I couldn't understand why. I don't know the exact premise, but for the bits and pieces I saw it was about a female boxer who ends up in the hospital or something like that. My father loves Clint Eastwood and old western flicks. He watches *The Good the Bad and the Ugly* consistently. Despite Mr. Eastwood's presence, I didn't see much killing or gunfighting. The movie seemed much more emotional which was usually taboo for my father. If it didn't have killing, shooting, blood, and guts, it wasn't for him.

The awkwardness between my father and I was reaching an uncomfortable level. I decided to be the bigger man and begin my apology.

"Dad, I'm sorry about not riding back with you. I was just frustrated and took it out on you. It was unfair and immature... I'm sorry."

My father said nothing. I had my head angled at the ground, for some reason my eyes refused to look at his when I apologized. The silence built up again, as a good minute or so went by with no response. I then picked my head up and looked at my father. He was starting to wipe his eyes with his index finger and thumb. Tears started to form as he visibly tried to keep them in. This was a man who once was called "the animal," by his peers. A man who worked eight to five every day and sometimes Saturdays if need be to make ends meet. He did grueling work as a plumber, always coming home with dirt under his fingernails and cuts on his arms. A man who wasn't supposed to cry.

"You okay, pops?" I got up and walked over resting my hand on his shoulder.

He was breathing hard and tears were now coming down like a severe rainstorm.

"I shouldn't have done it..." His hands remained over his face as he spoke short and sporadically.

"Dad what are you talking about? Shouldn't have done what?"

I looked at the T.V. and saw Clint Eastwood fiddling with wires on medical devices. He still had that trademark stone-faced look on his face; the look of a true tough guy. He then went back to look at the girl in the hospital bed, pushed the hair out of her face and gave her a light kiss on the forehead.

"She could've lived..." My father said.

The heart rate monitors on her machine began to beep slower and slower. Then they finally stopped beeping altogether. Clint Eastwood picked up his bag and walked out the room, down the hallway, and eventually out of the hospital. The screen went black and credits flashed on the screen.

I looked at my father. He had his whole hand covering his face now, breathing heavily in and then out.

"She could've made it... It's all my fault...I shouldn't have done it."

The words paralyzed me. My father never talked about his decision to cut my mom off life support. The doctors told us her status was not good and her level of pain would only get worse. My father had to make the tough decision but by all accounts the right one. Regardless I never knew the guilt that brewed inside of him. There was no more mystery now; his pain was my pain.

"No dad, it's not your fault. She was in so much pain there was no other choice."

I replaced my hand on his shoulder trying to ease his unnecessary burden.

"It was the right thing to do dad….the only thing to do."

I kept my hand on his shoulder, hoping for his tears to stop, but amazed by their presence at the same time.

"I just miss her so much." Pure, genuine sadness was pouring out of his eyes. He had not moved on. Like me he still loved her. He still needed her.

I was taken back by my father's rare trace of emotion, but I couldn't shake the image of him and Donna. Their "romance" was a slap in my mom's face. I believed my father's genuine sadness but questioned his recent actions at the same time.

"Dad, I have to ask, what about Donna?"

Finally, he removed his hand from his face wiping away the remaining moisture around his eyes and rose to his feet. He took a few deep breaths sniffling a few times in between. He placed his hand on my shoulder gently but securely at the same time.

"You have to understand, I loved your mother. Not a day goes by where I don't think about her. But, well…I guess it's just nice to have someone. I know it's not love, but it's something."

My father took his hand off my shoulder wiping his mouth as if he were searching for the right words to say.

"I want to show you something."

My father darted out of the room. He came back with a giant white photo album. I had been forced to look through them before with my mom and dad. It was a pretty painfully boring experience.

"Here are some photos of your mother and I when we were dating."

My father looked so young with his slicked back black hair, tight blue jeans, and expensive button-down shirt. It forced a smile on my face.

He flipped a few more pages until something flew out of the book landing on the floor beside us. I bent over and picked up the mysterious object. It was a mangled, dirty, synthetic white rose.

"Ah, that's what I gave your mother back when we started dating. Some guy at the supermarket sold it to me. He told me it was real but obviously, he was pulling my leg. Your mother knew right away."

I laughed thinking about how uncomfortable that situation must have been.

"Was she mad?"

"No, she just laughed and kissed me on the cheek. That's when I knew I had something special."

My father stared blankly at the page. I could tell his head was elsewhere in a reflection of a better time.

"I still can't believe she kept it for all those years."

He shook his head from side to side. A slight smile started to form.

"No one will ever be like your mother. She was a saint. We were lucky." I nodded my head.

" We certainly were."

There was a brief silence. A moment where there were no words but there didn't have to be. I felt like I understood more about my father in those three minutes than in my seventeen years on earth.

"Well, I'm gonna go to bed buddy," My father said, patting me on the shoulder.

"You sure you're okay?" I asked.

"Yeah, I am fine. I'll see you in the morning. I'll have breakfast waiting for you. I know you'll enjoy being able to eat something for a change."

Just like that he went right past me, opened the door to his bedroom, and closed it just as quickly.

I woke up the next day at 12:05. I must have been so tired my body needed a long rest. I was still thinking about last night. The image of my father crying was implanted in my head. It was an oxymoron that I couldn't ever figure out. I looked around the house but couldn't find my father anywhere. Finally, he walked in the door with a box of pizza in hand and Donna by his side. It was kind of a weird staple in my family but, we ate pizza any time.

"Good morning. How's my superstar wrestler feeling today?"

I was taken back by my father's lively manner. He hadn't displayed this much energy in a long time.

"Not bad pops... not bad at all," I said.

"Good to hear, I got us some pizza I figured we would watch the game and hang out for a while unless you got something going on?"

There was a vibrant look on my father's face and youthfulness in his voice. This was a side of him I had never seen before.

"Nope, I got nowhere else to be," I said.

"Awesome, come on, I think the games are about to start. You know if the Cowboys win they are in first place?"

I nodded my head and took a seat on the sofa I sat on last night. My father joined me in the same spot he was in last night as well. Donna was standing in between us awkwardly twirling her hair, visibly uncomfortable standing in between my father and I.

"Pete I should go. I have work in a few hours."

"Okay, well thanks for the pizza, I'll talk to you later tonight." My father gave her a hug and a light kiss on the lips.

I thought about Donna's pain. How it felt to lose her husband and try and move on. I wondered if she held it all in like my father did. I guess she needed someone like my father and my father needed someone like her. They were going through the same battle together.

"Thanks for the pizza, Donna," I said.

"No problem, James, I'll see you later."

Donna swiftly made her way out the door closing it forcefully behind her.

"You want a beer?" he asked.

"Sure."

He popped off the top of a Bud and handed it to me.

"Cheers buddy," he said.

"Cheers pops."

We lightly clanged our bottles together taking strong gulps in unison. I sat back on my sofa and let the smile appear on my face. I then directed my attention to the T.V. which contained a large white light taking up nearly half the screen.

"Wow, talk about a huge glare. Let me take care of it."

My dad slowly walked over to the window pulling down the shades and sat back down. For a moment it looked like all of the light was gone, but there looked like there was a small spec of light that still remained. It was so small, I wondered if it was even really there.

Chapter 21
Love

Things at home weren't much better. It felt like a maze. He knew he deserved some distance for irresponsible behavior. He got really drunk and his wife was pregnant and stone-cold sober. It was not good, especially for a soon to be father approaching 30 years old. He expected the cold shoulder and some distance, but this was different. She hugged him and held him. They opened that envelope and shared a moment not just as husband and wife, but as a mother and father. In some ways, they were closer than ever, but they were also so far apart.

"I have to go to school," Coach told Rachel.

She nodded. "Okay, have a good day. I love you,"

He leaned in for a kiss and at first it felt like it had almost ten years ago when they first started dating. When he walked her to her front door and mustered the courage to put his hand on her waist and go in for the kiss. He was never very successful with women. He had kissed girls before, but he was very timid, unconfident. He was always very careful and calculated and unsure if his moves her right. Were they too strong? Not strong enough? So when Rachel embraced his hand on her waist and turned her head to the side, ever so slightly, inviting his lips to access hers, it gave him this inner warmth that undeniably blissful. She had light green eyes that seemed to almost radiate when he looked at them. They were gorgeous, but it was beyond their beauty; there was something deeper than that. They seemed to ignite when he stared deeply into them, and he felt like the most important person in her life. The only thing she cared about above all else.

That feeling subsides with marriage and time, but that fire never fully went out. Sometimes when they kissed it was a burning inferno. Other times it was a couple embers that felt barely lit. After nights where he stayed out too late with his friends, or she nagged him about completing projects around the house— no matter the fight or disagreement, the fire remained.

Now, he hated to say it, but when he held her and gave her that kiss the fire was missing. Nothing he could identify specifically. He still thought she was beautiful pregnant and all. He loved being around her and loved having her close to him, but things were different now, and it was undeniable. Maybe it was the way her body tensed up a bit anytime he got close to her. Her arms got a bit stiff and robotic. Her face was almost expressionless and without the same color and vibrance. It was like she not really there with him, off somewhere in her head that was miles and miles away. He would lean in for a kiss, and her eyes were glaring straight ahead, without that same light and flicker that he got so used to. The same light that made him fall in love with her. Those eyes were now lifeless focusing on something far past him.

"I love you too," he replied as he rubbed her back gently. He meant that. He did love her and would always, but he felt uneasy, to say the least. He couldn't help but wonder for the first time if she really did love him.

He slowly got in his car and drove to work with that question carrying in his head the entire ride.

Chapter 22
Playoffs Practice

Coach V got a text message from the athletic director of the league. It was short and to the point and revealed what he already knew, the Cougars were in the playoffs. They had moved from one of the worst teams in the league to the number two team in the city. Their matchup was going to be on Saturday against Fairleigh. Coach felt great about what the team had done this season, but he felt even better about their chances to win on Saturday and perhaps, win the championship.

To say practice went poorly would be an understatement. Much of the team showed up fifteen minutes late. They walked in laughing, eating bags of chips, and drinking soda. Being a wrestler throughout high school, Coach always talked about the importance of nutrition. He was not stupid, he knew that many of the families struggle to put food on the table, especially in New Haven. However, he felt obligated to tell his guys to avoid sugar and sodium. He referenced some of the best athletes and how important their diet was. It rarely worked and it was a battle he didn't feel like having today. The team after all was on a roll and he felt maybe they deserved a little fun.

"How we doing fellas," Coach said as they walked by.

"Doing good coach," Terrell was the one to respond as they made their way to the trailer to get changed.

Their equipment was kept in the trailer. It was about a 100-foot-wide metal crate that was kept outside. Each player put their stuff on the floor in a designated spot. It was not the best system. He would have preferred a locker room, but they made do with it.

Usually, it took them five minutes to get ready, ten at the most, but today it had been fifteen minutes and still, they were not ready.

He heard laughing and yelling and cussing and he was starting to get frustrated. He made it a point not to go into the trailer unless he had to for obvious reasons.

"Hurry up! Let's go! We got a playoff game to get ready for!"

He was hoping that would be enough to get them ready, but as soon as he left the trailer there was more laughing, more yelling, and more fooling around.

It took them almost a half hour to get ready.

Coach brought the team into a circle. You could feel the energy was at a low. The kids were walking to the huddle. Their heads cocked to a side. Something was wrong.

"Listen, guys, we got a playoff game this Saturday. We got five days to get ready. Our focus, our attitude, our effort has got to be dialed in this week."

He looked at his guys hoping to see them looking at him and matching his focus, but instead, he saw many of them with their heads down, playing with grass or their equipment. He shook his head. He felt like screaming, felt like throwing something to wake them up, but he decided against it.

"We cannot take that long to get ready this week. Ten minutes at the most. Then we are out here ready to stretch and go."

He paused and studied the faces. A couple were looking at him. Freddy, Vinny, but Lito and Terrell had their eyes elsewhere. They were seemingly staring at something in the distance, somewhere that was not here.

"Okay, hard work on three."

They broke the huddle and coach prayed practice would get them woken up and focused.

He was wrong.

To say it was one of the worst practices they had would be a gross understatement. Their stretches were lethargic and uninspired. Their blocking consisted of T-rex arms and patty cake. Their tackling looked more like hugs.

"Anyone want to play today!" Coach yelled.

"If we don't show some goddamn effort, we are going to run for the rest of practice."

He wanted to go over plays. He wanted to review their defense and offensive strategy, but this could not happen if they wanted to fool around and not practice hard.

Terrell took the snap and threw a toss to Lito. The toss was placed right into his hands in almost the perfect spot, not too high or too low, but right at his helmet so he could catch and turn upfield. Lito grabbed it but didn't have the same burst as normal. Coach had seen Lito run countless times now, and when he wanted to be he was one of the fastest players in the league. Not this time. Vinny came down field like he was taught. He changed his level, squared his shoulders, and was running full speed. Lito made a crucial mistake, which he rarely ever did. He stopped. A cardinal sin for any player. If you stop you are like a stalled car on the train tracks. Sometimes professionals get away with it, but most of the time it ends very, very poorly. This was one of those times. Vinny delivered a hit that was so textbook, so perfect. His head was up and to the side, his arms were wrapped around Lito's torso, and he drove right into Lito's chest. The hit gave an audible pop as it was delivered and Lito was driven back three to four feet as he fell to the ground almost like he was apart of a car crash. The team fell silent for what felt like an eternity.

"What the heck bro!" Lito said as he popped up to his feet. He pushed Vinny in the chest and then raised a hand to his facemask.

"What's your problem! You wanna go?" Lito shrugged his shoulders and squared himself up as if he was expecting retaliation. Vinny stood his ground. He didn't say a word, did not charge or do anything really.

Still the team raced over and circled them quickly. They were expecting something to happen and so was Coach.

"Hey, hey, what the hell is wrong with you?!" Coach got in between Lito and Vinny but was facing right at Lito.

"This dude does too much," Lito was clearly upset. His voice was tense and his body was tenser.

Coach had enough.

"Vinny delivered a clean hit and did exactly what you are supposed to do, if you were running hard and not like twinkle toes then this wouldn't happen."

A couple of the boys laughed. He didn't mean to insult Lito, but he wanted to send a message. this was not okay. Vinny played hard and delivered. a clean hit. Lito was not taking it seriously and something bad happened.

"You're always taking his side Coach!"

"What are you talking about?"

"You never get on him, you never say anything to him, but you're always on me."

That was not true or fair. Coach took that personally. He did the best he could to treat everyone fairly. He did the best he could to be honest.

"That's just not true. I---"

"No, no it is,"

Lito took off his helmet and began to shake his head side to side.

"Okay bring it in."

The boys slowly took their helmets off and walked casually to his spot.

"Now!" Coach yelled with as much force as he could muster.

The boys got visibly faster in their effort to get to his spot.

"Look, we have come a long way. We have worked hard and made our way to the playoffs when no one gave us a shot."

He paused dramatically trying to let that sink in.

"But, that is all we are going to do if we don't work hard and cut this crap out."

He looked around and there seemed to be more faces looking at him now.

"If we halfway do things. If we halfway run, halfway tackle, halfway play, then we are going to get our asses kicked. Plain and simple."

Silence.

"If we fool around in the trailer, giggling and play around, and take freaking 30 minutes to get ready like it's some prom date, then we are going to get our asses kicked."

His face felt hotter and his neck was getting tense and he couldn't stop himself.

"You guys gotta ask yourselves if you are okay with being average, being okay, being just another team that loses. People saying, they tried hard, they were pretty good, but not good enough. That is not okay with me."

He paused again and took a deep breath.

"If you want to be part of this family, you need to be here on time, work hard, and get rid of whatever this was today." He turned around and pointed at the field.

"Are you guys ready to do that?" Coach asked.

There were some "yes coach" responses, but many stayed silent.

"Are we ready to do that?"

"Yes, Coach!" Almost all responded. Coach looked at Vinny. His head was up and he was looking right at him. Lito's head was down staring at the ground or grass.

"Okay, let's break it down and get ready to work tomorrow."

They broke it down with a little more energy than they showed at practice. Maybe it was just a bad day.

"Lito, Vinny, come see me for a minute."

They walked over dragging their feet to his spot. Coach was between both of them as they faced him.

"Look, I need to know you guys are straight. Things happens out here. We get fired up, we go hard and then tempers flare."

Lito had his helmet on his hip, his face cocked to one side in a very subtle form of defiance.

"We are going to need both of you in order to win this thing. Are you guys cool? Are we straight?"

Vinny nodded, but Lito said nothing. Did nothing.

"Lito, you cool?"

There was a pause and finally, he responded.

"I guess."

"Okay, let's shake hands and get ready for tomorrow."

Vinny offered his hand almost immediately. Lito inspected it for a good ten seconds. Coach was about to say something to encourage him when Lito finally stuck his hand out and shook it. It was a weak floppy handshake, but it was a handshake, nonetheless.

"Okay, good. Get changed and get out of here and get ready for tomorrow."

Vinny jogged to the trailer, while Lito walked gingerly with his helmet in his hand.

Chapter 23
Playoffs Practice II

Maybe the talk yesterday worked because right at 3:30 almost the entire team was in the trailer and was changing. There was no fooling around. No fake fighting, running around, or joking. It was a small victory on the surface, but Coach couldn't help but feel vindicated. He felt respected, listened to. Part of him wondered if this team-- their talent, abilities-- if it could win without him. He had that thought from time to time and he had the need to swat it away like a nagging fly, but it never ever went away.

The entire team was changed and on the field within seven minutes. Coach nodded his head in appreciation. He didn't say anything as they each confidently walked to their spots for warmups, but he clearly did not have to. There was energy in their movements. Leg kicks went a little higher, sprints that seemed a little faster, maybe it was his imagination, but things seemed better. The intensity, focus, and attitude all seemed right where it needed to be for them to be successful.

It took Coach a minute, but he realized something was wrong. It was Vinny. Vinny was not there. Attendance was a problem for some, but never for Vinny. He was almost always on time and one of the guys he could count on to bring it every day. After stretches, Vinny was jogging to the trailer over twenty minutes late. The team got water and returned to Coach as Vinny attempted to enter the huddle. Coach's eyes almost magnetized to Lito. He could feel the glare from Lito that spoke silent volumes. He remembered their conversation yesterday.

"You never say anything to him. You always take his side."

He didn't remember the exact words, but he knew exactly what Lito meant. He thought it was unfair and untrue. Vinny never gave him a reason to get on his case, until now.

"What's up Vinny, why are you so late?"

Coach tried to walk a tightrope of firm but understanding.

Vinny shrugged his shoulders at the question. That wasn't the worst response, but it was close. He took a quick look at the team huddled together in a semi-circle. He could tell that they were all waiting to see what would happen. That this was a moment of trial. What was Coach going to say? What was Coach going to do?

"Vinny, you gotta give me something? You are over twenty minutes late to practice the week we got a playoff game. Is someone dying? Are you sick? What the hell is it?"

There was a pause. Coach did feel bad that he called Vinny out in front of the team. That was not his style, but he did give Vinny a chance and he didn't take it.

It felt like ages of silence. It was hard to say how long exactly, but long enough where Coach was about to ask him again. Something like "well," or "what do you have to say?" When Vinny finally responded.

"I had to go through Grove Street."

Coach did not know every street in New Haven, but he knew Grove was the long way to the field from school. It was much shorter to go right down the Boulevard. That was what most if not all of the team did all the time.

"Why? Why not the Boulevard like everyone else?" It was an awkward feeling in the air. It felt like an interrogation, but Coach was honestly curious now.

"I had to go home first and then come here. My mom called and needed me."

Coach halfway accepted that answer. It might have been a personal situation and there was no point in bringing that up out in the open.

"Well, please let me know next time. Where do you live?" Coach was more curious than anything.

"Off Marshall, by the repair shop."

Coach did not know New Haven very well, but he knew that area a bit. There was a street.. What was it called… he racked his brain to think of the name, but it was connected to the Boulevard and it seemed much shorter.

The team must have thought the conversation was over as many started to strap their helmets to check their shoelaces, but Coach remembered the name of the street.

"Wait, why didn't you take Truman? Doesn't it connect right to the Boulevard? It'd bring you right here?"

There was silence and he wondered if he said something incorrect. He retraced his steps in his head and thought again and he was pretty sure his geography was right.

There were awkward looks from the boys. Some shook their heads. Some gave smirks and shared glances. It was like there was something on Coach's face, or behind his back and he didn't know it, but it was clear as day to them. Coach began to realize that his suggestion demonstrated how little he knew and he felt stupid for even trying.

"Okay, well I need five sprints Vinny. We need to be focused and be here on time. That goes for all of you. We need to be here and be ready. We got a playoff game Saturday and we need to be ready."

Vinny nodded and did not protest as he jogged to the line to begin his sprints.

Lito walked over to him with his helmet in his hand and was ready to hear how awful or unfair he was. He braced himself and searched his brain for comments and retorts.

"Coach, no one goes down Truman unless you live there."

Coach nodded. At that moment Coach felt more like an outsider than he had before. He was not from this world and if that was in doubt it was not anymore.

"Thanks. Get some water and then let's get ready to roll today."

Lito walked off to the water container as Vinny reached down to tap the white line, turn around and run back. He was running hard as if there were defenders all over him and the end zone was clearly in sight. He had four more to do before practice started.

Chapter 24
Vinny

Vinny was covered in sweat and dirt. He was running late from practice and was supposed to be home ten minutes ago. He burst into the door almost out of breath.

"You are late." his mom said, with his youngest brother latched to her chest.

He had three other brothers that were all younger each separated by a little over a year.

"I can't be late to work or that is it for me."

Vinny nodded. He heard the speech before, but he always did the best he could, leaving practice right as he could and running home even though his legs were dead tired and his energy was practically zero.

"Sorry, mama. I got here as quickly as I could."

She sighed.

"We cannot do this. I need your help Vin. If I lose this job we lose everything…"

He nodded. He knew his mom had to work to pay the bills and she was doing the best she could and the last thing he wanted to do was let her down.

"I know you love football, but family comes first."

She stuck out her finger and pointed it right at his chest.

"It always comes first."

She handed him baby Hector without a warning or asking as she left the room.

Hector cried almost instantly as he was in Vinny's arms. Vinny watched Hector every day and thought maybe Hector would be used to him by now, but that was not the case. Hector missed his mom I guess and there was not much Vinny could do. He rocked Hector back and forth with gradual intensity.

Bruce and Juan were playing video games on the floor with their legs crossed and eyes glued to the TV.

"Homework?" Vinny asked his brothers.

"Yeah, after this game," Bruce said.

"No, now, let's go!"

"You do your homework and I'll play the next game." Juan reached for the controller.

"The hell you are!"

Bruce and Juan battled in a moderate level intensity wrestling match for the controller. No punches, but Juan reached for the controller as Bruce kept it as a safe unreachable distance in the air.

Vinny snuck behind Bruce and grabbed the controller with the opposite hand as he kept the crying Hector in the other.

"Okay, my controller, let's go. Upstairs to do your work."

His brothers muttered something under their breath and marched to their rooms. Hector's crying was lessening to whimpers until it almost was totally gone.

His mom came down the stairs with her hair up and her apron on.

"I have a double tonight, so I won't be back until tomorrow morning. Make sure you give Hector a bath and the boys don't stay up too late."

He knew the drill, but his mom always felt the need to repeat it.

Vinny nodded his head.

His mom leaned in and gave him a kiss on the forehead, and then one to Hector.

"I love you. Remember, family always first," she patted him on the head and rubbed his hair behind his ear as she grabbed her bag and left.

Hector cried almost instantly after the door closed and his mom rushed out to go to work.

Chapter 25
Playoffs

It was game day. Coach woke up early like he normally did and got ready. He put on his black sweatpants, long sleeve hoodie, and packed all the coaching gear in his car.

He went downstairs to check on his wife, but she was still fast asleep. He debated about giving her a kiss. He had done this almost every time he left. He got as far as to lean down and puck his lips, but for some reason, he stopped when he was around five inches from her. Even under oath, he wouldn't be able to explain what stopped him from doing this, but it happened. He turned and went upstairs, got in his car, and left for the field.

He got there very early, much earlier than anyone else on the team. He liked it that way. He was able to go over the plays he liked, and think about what would be best in a game like this. He would be lying if he said he was not nervous. He was very nervous, but he tried not to let anyone see it.

Finally, the team arrived in waves. They got changed at a moderate pace, but there was a clearer sense of focus. Very little to no fooling around from anyone, with a couple of the reserve players cracking jokes and chasing each other. Vinny,

Terrell, and Lito were all focused. They stood confidently on the field stretching their arms and legs and chatting quietly on the side.

"Vinny, can you come here for a second?"

Vinny slowly jogged over with his head down as he made his way to coach.

"I want to apologize for challenging you yesterday. You have been a great teammate and we could not have gotten here without you."

Vinny was looking down, but he nodded slightly.

"I want to thank you for everything. I mean that."

Coach patted Vinny on the back of the helmet.

"We good?"

Vinny nodded again. This time much more confidently.

"We good, Coach."

They got to the field first, which was a huge plus. They were able to review some of their bread and butter plays. The tosses, handoffs, sweeps, and basic pass plays. Coach liked the intensity, focus, and determination that each of them showed. It was the little things mostly. The way they broke the huddle and got quickly to the line of scrimmage. The way they got into their stances with good balance and eyes focused on the football. The team felt ready.

Fairleigh arrived perfectly after they got through their warmups.

Coach had a pretty good idea about what Fairleigh had. They had a quarterback who was the coach's son, a solid wideout in 88 and that was about it, but as the team went to the sideline he noticed new players he had not seen before. Two athletes that were average height, but looked to be very athletic, and one very big kid who Coach would have definitely remembered when they played the first time.

The other big difference were the number of coaches. Last time they played it was the one coach and his assistant. They were jeans and polo shirts. Both had dreads that stuck out the ends of their hats. They both had Timberland boots on their feet and big chains. This time there were at least five more coaches or parents or something on the sideline. Coach began to feel a little uneasy and the players seemed to notice.

"Coach! They got new players!" Lito said pointing to their sideline.

"Don't worry about them. I got it."

Lito shook his head and sucked his teeth in frustration.

Coach got his team together for a quick speech.

"Listen, it doesn't matter who they got on that side."

Coach said as he pointed behind them to Fairleigh.

"All that matters is we handle what we need to. If we each do our jobs--" he pointed across at all of the players one by one.

"Then we got nothing to worry about. Let's ball out!"

They broke down the huddle and went to their sideline.

***

Fairleigh won the toss and got the ball first.

195

Right away they put the new kids into action. The big kid was in the backfield and he was given the ball on a fullback dive. He was a little too big to be a conventional running back, but it worked well. His first carry went for nearly fifteen yards as two or three defenders could not get him down. They ran the same play again for another first down of at least a ten-yard gain. Coach called a double A gap blitz to try and stop the run, but the Fairleigh coach seemed to expect this. Instead of giving the ball to the big boy the QB kept the ball and rolled out to the right. There was only one defender there and it was Vinny. Vinny squared up on the quarterback, he made a crucial error of guessing where the QB would go and dove to the right instead of reading him. That caused him to miss badly as the QB run to the end zone for a touchdown.

"Keep your heads up! We're gonna get the ball and score!" Coach noticed some frustration from his guys but was hoping to motivate them to stay focused. There was a lot of football left.

On the kickoff the Coach elected to go for a bold, almost crazy call. An onside kick. If it didn't work, the ball would be on the 35-yard line and a short field for them to work with. But the kick was executed pretty well. It was a bouncy ball that hit off Freddy's helmet and bounced backward right into the arms of a Fairleigh defender. Fairleigh got the ball right back.

Their sideline erupted. Kids jumping up and down and the parents and coaches high fiving and jumping up and down wildly.

"Defense, let's go! Get a stop."

Unfortunately, a stop they did not get. Coach stacked the box expecting another run. Vinny came hard on a blitz and was in perfect position to make the sack, but he whiffed, diving again for the quarterback's legs and missing. The quarterback shook off Vinny and then threw a wobbly, but catchable ball to number 88 who was wide open. The result was a touchdown and a quick 14 nothing deficit for the Cougars.

"Vinny, what the hell is wrong with you! Can't you tackle anyone!" Lito shouted as loud as possible.

"Hey, that's not going to help! You do your job and Vinny will do his! Let's score this drive and were right back in it."

Unfortunately, the drive did not start well. On the first play, there was a fumbled snap that almost cost them the ball. Luckily, Terrell dove on it to save the ball. The next play was a sloppy handoff to Lito that went for no gain. Their third play was a false start.

"They ain't nothing! They nervous. Attack 'em boys! Attack!" Their coach was shouting to his guys. It was one thing to try to rile up your guys, but it was another to attack kids. Calling them soft, or being demeaning was so unprofessional.

"Lito come here!" Lito shook his head but jogged over.

"I'm giving you the toss here, run your ass off and get in that end zone. You hear me?!" Lito nodded. Coach tried to be as forceful and as aggressive as he could. He stared at the other sideline and hoped he could channel his rage to Lito.

For some reason, the Fairleigh coach called an all-out blitz. Maybe he felt aggressive, maybe he was going in for the kill, or maybe he was just not smart. Whatever the reason, it worked out perfectly for them. The blitz came and the toss to the right went right into Lito's hands. Lito took the ball to the edge easily running to the sideline avoiding all the defenders. Lito ran down the opposing sideline and even waved at the coaches and parents as he made his way into the end zone. They erupted.

"Penalty! Taunting! That is bull!"

"Lito! Come here!"

Lito jogged over with a smile on his face.

"Don't pull that again, you focus on the game, don't worry about them at all. You got me?"

"But Coach they are talking mad junk."

"I know, but if you do it to then we got nothing to go on. I need you to trust me and just play. Don't get into it."

Lito did the slightest of nods.

"Heck of a run," Coach said as he playfully hit Lito on the helmet in congratulations.

Fairleigh got the ball back and was moving right around their 30-yard line. Coach called a time out. Coach gambled and called the same blitz as before.

"Vinny, you are going to be free, I need you to make the tackle. Look at the QB's hips, keep your head up and tackle. I trust you. You got it?"

Vinny nodded as Coach saw Lito roll his eyes. Coach ignored him.

Sure enough, Vinny got through the line and had a clear shot at the quarterback. The QB was dead to rights but got greedy. He tried to sidestep Vinny like he did before leaving the ball far away from his body. This was a terrible decision and it cost him. The ball popped out like the top of a soda can. Lito was in perfect position to pick it up and go all the way to the end zone for a touchdown. Tied game at half time.

The Fairleigh quarterback returned to his sideline with his head down and hands on his hips.

The Fairleigh coach was furious, jabbing his finger into his chest with intensity. Coach V could not make out the words, but it was definitely not a pep talk.

The rest of the Fairleigh team had similar body language. Their heads were down and they lumbered slowly to the sideline with little intensity or aggression. Coach V knew what it looked like to give up, and they had it written all over them.

Coach V was so distracted that he barely noticed Lito dancing in the end zone. He was gyrating his hips and swinging his arms as he pointed at the Fairleigh sideline.

"Lito! Get over here!"

The ref ran up to Coach V.

"Coach that should be a penalty, I am going to give a warning this time, but keep that in mind."

Coach nodded, "Thank you, it won't happen again."

High fives, fist bumps, those were fine, but dancing and showing up your opponent was not appropriate and it was not good sportsmanship. Coach did not want to teach that or allow it.

Lito ran back not even looking at the coach.

"Woah, woah, hang on a second. Don't pull that crap again you hear me?"

"Coach chill, just having fun…"

"You do that again you are on the bench you hear me?"

Lito walked by without saying a word. Coach didn't bother responding, hoping he got his point across.

The Cougars got the ball after halftime. On their very first play Coach called a pass play. Terrell could hit Vinny or Lito depending on who was open. There was also the option for him to keep it and run himself. The Fairleigh coach did not blitz so when Terrell dropped back he had time, but no one seemed open. Terrell rolled out to his left with defenders closing in. It seemed like an eternity that Terrell had the ball. He made it almost to the sideline before releasing the ball. It landed right in the hands of Vinny. Somehow the defenders lost Vinny or left him uncovered, thinking that there was no way Terrell could get it to him, but he could and he did. Vinny caught the ball and ran all the way to the end zone untouched.

Coach was so proud of the great play by Terrell he gave him a hug. He patted him on the helmet and was jumping up and down.

"Heck of a job Terrell! Great play!"

Through the chaos Coach then saw the yellow flag on the ground and Lito with his helmet off.

The ref sprinted in between Lito and a Fairleigh defender. The Fairleigh players was short and stocky. You don't always want to judge ability by size, but this kid was not one of their better players. Coach was trying to sort out what happened. When the ref returned to the sideline with Lito.

"Coach, we had two players fighting, I'm supposed to suspend both, but I think it's best if we just eject them both and continue. No suspensions if they can keep it together."

Lito shot his arms in the air and stomped his feet.

"Coach! He hit me right in the face! He started that! What am I supposed to do?"

Coach V was furious. He talked about being smarter than to do something stupid like fighting. Talk with your pads was always his message. He was about to lash out at Lito..

"It's true Coach, the other kids socked Lito from behind. It was a total cheap shot," one of the players added.

Coach V, looked at the ref who was still standing there.

"I didn't see that. I just saw them both going at each other. I have to kick them both out Coach, or it can get more serious. What do you want to do?"

Coach looked across the sideline and saw the Fairleigh coach give the short stocky kid a fist bump and pat on the helmet as if to signify "good job." Coach V quickly realized what had happened. The Fairleigh coach used one of his worse players to bait Lito into a trap. Lito took it hook line and sinker and now he was out for the rest of the game.

Coach nodded reluctantly and Lito slammed his helmet on the ground in frustration. They would have to continue without him.

Coach V was still very new to coaching football, but one thing he figured out was you couldn't force things. Keeping it simple was best. A bunch of plays sounds great, and they might even look great in practice, but it takes a while for kids to learn them and they usually don't execute well in the pressure of a game. The Fairleigh coach began to fall in the trap of trying crazy things. He tried a double re-verse that got bobbled and almost caused a fumble. Then he tried a flea-flicker where the big kid took two steps forward after a handoff and then tossed it back to the QB. The prob-lem was their defense was right there and the QB barely had time to catch the ball, let alone make a throw.

Luckily for Coach V and the Cougars, these trick plays wasted almost the entire third quarter. The problem was the Cougars couldn't score either. Their defense keyed in on Terrell and Vinny. They were double covering Vinny, and Terrell couldn't get him the ball. Without Lito, their offense was very one dimensional and the Fairleigh coach knew it.

The fourth quarter started and for some reason the Fairleigh coach woke up. He began to call more traditional plays. He ran the ball up the middle with the big running back for a ten-yard gain. The next play he did a fake hand off to the big kid and the quarterback scrambled outside the pocket for a 20 yards. Then he called a toss play to the running back with the big boy lead blocking. The toss was perfect and the big boy blocked well as the Fairleigh running back ran all the way into the end zone untouched. All those plays going to the right side where Lito should be.

It was now a tied game in the fourth quarter and Coach had to find a way to score. He kept up with the basics. He ran tosses to Vinny and quarterback keep runs with Terrell. They registered modest gains, but the Fairleigh coach began to be more aggressive. He was now sending more blitzes and pressures. On the next two plays, they went backward and it was now third down. Coach called a timeout.

"They are keying in on you two," Coach said as he pointed at Vinny and Terrell.

Coach thought about it and he decided to go with an unconventional play. He had no other choice really.

"Okay, we are going to call a tight end screen."

They only practiced the play a handful of times, but it was something Coach liked. It had looked okay in practice, a bit sloppy, but not awful.

"Without Lito, we are going to fake the toss to the right with Vinny, then we are going to hit Freddy right in the middle with blockers in front. All you gotta do Freddy is catch the ball and run like hell. Got it?"

Freddy nodded. His eyes perked up and you could tell he was excited to get the ball.

They broke the huddle and got lined up. Terrell took the snap and faked the toss perfectly to Vinny. The entire Fairleigh team bit on the fake, moving all the way to the right and Terrell had Freddy wide open in the middle of the field. But Terrell did not throw it to him. Instead, he kept the ball himself and ran to the outside. He made good progress and got the first down before getting shoved out of bounds inside the twenty-five-yard line. They had a first down, but there were only fifteen seconds left. Coach called another time out.

"What happened?!" Coach asked Terrell as they were on the sideline.

"You had Freddy wide open!"

Terrell shrugged his shoulders.

"Coach he can't catch."

Freddy instantly hung his head in defeat.

"Listen, you execute the plays I call, okay?"

Terrell stuck his hands out as if to say "okay."

They needed twenty-five yards; Coach had to call a pass play.

"Okay, we need to pass. I am going to have you run a corner route, Vinny. The other guys are going to run quick outs. Terrell, if Vinny is covered don't force it."

Terrell nodded.

"What about me Coach?" Freddy asked.

"I really need you to block bud. Can you do that?" Freddy nodded as he stropped his helmet along with the rest of the team and jogged on the field.

Terrell took the snap and dropped back. Coach froze. The Fairleigh coach called a blitz from Terrell's blindside. Terrell was looking at Vinny's direction he didn't see it. Somehow he just managed to swing his head around in time to recognize the defender at the last moment. He moved just enough to avoid getting killed, but the Fairleigh defender grabbed him by the waist and was twirling him toward the ground. Quarterbacks are taught to protect the ball at all costs. Coach always preached that. Keep the ball high and tight, close to your body. Terrell broke that rule. He had the ball out in his arms away from his body, breaking all proper football logic. For some reason, Freddy was right in front of Terrell. It is hard to tell if it was on purpose, instincts, or just pure luck, but Terrell managed to hand the ball to Freddy as he was going to the ground. The ball was in Freddy's hands as Terrell hit the ground violently on his backside. Luckily the chaotic scene was so hard to follow. No one knew Freddy had the ball. Freddy ran to the left side and there was no one there. All the defenders had their back turned guarding Vinny expecting the ball to go to him. Freddy ran as fast as he could, which as not particularly fast, but luckily on this occasion, it did not have to be. By the time the Fairleigh defenders smarted up to what was happening it was too late. Freddy was right at the goal line and managed to score.

They all erupted. Engulfing Freddy with hugs and celebrations. Coach was jumping up and down and hugging his guys and giving wild high fives. They had done it. They had won the playoff game and were headed to the championship.

Coach trotted on the field as he looked at Freddy with a smile ear to ear and the football high above his head. He looked like a totally different person as teammates surrounded him patting him on the shoulder pads and back shouting, "We going to the ship!"

Over and over again.

They quickly lined up and got ready to shake hands with the opposing team. Coach began to realize how dangerous this could be. He did not want anyone to do something stupid, like throw a punch or say something that would create a problem.

"All you say is good game, you hear me?" A couple responded.

"I said you hear me?"

"Yes, Coach!"

The handshake line went fine with Coach V in the back. He noticed the Fairleigh Coach very animated as he shook hands, but he couldn't make out what it was he was saying.

As he got closer he heard it

"Shake my damn hand man!"

"Look me in the damn eyes son!"

Coach V could see the Fairleigh coach shaking a bit and his eyes were a bit red.

"Coach, easy. You okay."

"Oh, I'm straight. You lucky you got this one on us. Some bull is all I got to say."

The Fairleigh coach nodded. He knew the Fairleigh coach wanted a response, but Coach V refused to take the bait.

"Great game coach. Thank you."

He shook his hand and turned to return to his sideline. As he jogged, he looked up and noticed a familiar figure in the stands. It was the Barrett coach with his arms folded across his chest. It was hard to make him out in the distance, but Coach could tell for sure it was him. Coach V jogged a bit quicker to the sideline getting ready to talk to his players about the championship game only one week away.

Chapter 26
Championship Practice

Coach spent the whole car ride home thinking about the game. In one way he was so proud of what they had done. In his very first year as head coach, his team was headed to the championship. They came from behind, they fought and now they were headed to the big game. He was not a very emotional guy. He rarely cried, not because he was super tough, but just because. He was not quite crying as he pulled onto the highway and got ready to head home, but his eyes were swelling up a bit and his cheeks burned.

There was the other side though. They had barely won that game. He also thought about Lito. How he lost control for a bit and got out of his game. He knew that was going to be a problem if they could not fix it before this weekend.

Coach pulled into the driveway and walked inside. Rachel was there in the kitchen making what looked like chicken parm.

"That looks fantastic," Coach said as he gave her a hug and rubbed her stomach.

"Thanks. She leaned back slightly to give him a peck on the cheek."

"How'd the game go?"

"We won. We are going to the championship." Coach said as he grabbed a water from the fridge.

"Oh wow! That's awesome! I am so proud of you."

When he closed the fridge door, she was right in front of him. She extended her arms and gave him a big hug. Her stomach with his future daughter was hard pressed against his. It was a middle school championship game in one city out of hundreds in CT, and it was a small hug in the many they had shared in their ten years together, but for some reason, it felt like so much more. He held her tightly with both hands squeezing with careful strength. His eyes welled up again as he held her close for longer than she probably expected, but she didn't pull away. They shared a kiss in the kitchen. A closed mouth, lips puckered kiss, as he continued to hold her. It was not perfect, but it was something.

"Thank you," was all Coach managed to sneak out. Followed by "I love you."

"I love you too," she responded as they finally let go and got ready for dinner.

Dinner was great. The chicken parm had Rachel's fantastic sauce. The chicken was just crispy enough, and the cheese was just enough to compliment the chicken but not dominate. Coach opened a bottle of wine during dinner and talked about their future daughter. What she might look like and how she might act. They smiled throughout the entire conversation.

"I have to ask, how are you doing?"

There was a pause. An invisible discomfort to the question. It clearly startled her and he immediately regretted the comment..

"I'm okay." was all she managed to get out as she took a sip of water.

"I wanted to tell you again how sorry I am for everything. I really feel awful for what I put you through."

Coach immediately regretted bringing this up. They were having a good day and he just couldn't help, but ruin it.

"It... it is not that honestly," she paused, looking down at her wine glass and then at the ground.

"I just feel different. I can't explain it. I just don't feel like myself."

Rachel wiped her face, but she was not crying.

Coach thought about what to say next or how to respond, but he blanked.

"I am sorry, I have no idea what you are going through. I just wanted you to know that I really want to help. I mean that."

Rachel nodded. "I understand, but it is not your fault. Honestly, I thought about it a lot and it is really me."

She paused and looked around as if the words were somewhere around her.

"It is just me. I don't know. I just feel different. I can't explain it, but it is not about you or the drinking or anything like that. It is just me."

Coach nodded but was still very confused.

"Just know that I love you and I want to help you any way that I can and however I can."

Rachel nodded. "Thank you."

Coach took the plates and glasses and cleaned them in the kitchen. They watched a movie and had a little more wine and things felt closer to normal than he thought.

They both went upstairs to get ready for bed. They brushed their teeth and washed their faces. There was a bit of an awkward silence as they got ready. Neither of them spoke until Coach got the nerve to say something.

"So, would you want to maybe try sleeping up here tonight.?" Rachel paused for a moment.

"I.. I'm just not ready yet. I'm sorry."

Coach nodded.

"Okay, I understand."

"I'm sorry."

"It's okay. I can sleep downstairs tonight." Coach said.

"No, no I can go," Rachel replied.

"I don't mind. You take the bed tonight."

Rachel shrugged her shoulders. "You sure?"

"I'm sure."

Coach V leaned in for a kiss and a hug.

"I love you," she said.

"I love you too."

Then Coach left the bedroom to go down to the couch to get some sleep.

Chapter 27
Rachel

Rachel replayed the image again and again in her head. Almost seven months ago, she looked down at that stick the size of a thermometer and read those words in clear black font: *pregnant.* It was all she ever wanted her entire life— to be a mother. It was something she dreamed about since she was a little girl, pushing her Barbie and American girl dolls around the house in the stroller. She would carefully color coordinate their outfits making sure their tops matched their bottoms, and their bottoms matched their shoes. She carefully combed their hair with the small brush and cleaned what dirt was on their faces or bodies.

But now that her little girl was about to be here things felt different. This was the moment she had imagined her entire life, the image she pictured forever, and for some unknown reason, she couldn't shake this feeling of discomfort. A dark, unsettling feeling that crept up on her and took over. It was so strong that she had to lie down sometimes and pull the covers up to her chin. She wasn't sleeping great. Sometimes she woke up at night in a cold sweat and had trouble going back to sleep. The worst part about it was she had no idea why.

It hadn't always been this way. When she was a young girl, she had dreamed of performing. She performed mini - shows in front of her dad and mom that were always captured on an old school video camera. The film was grainy and hard to see, but in a way that contributed to the charm. Rachel would pop out on the screen with an electric smile, adorable chubby cheeks and wild outfits of oversized sunglasses and electric dresses. She sang original songs that were a little off key, dance moves that weren't quite on rhythm, but her energy and resilience to never stop was engaging and encouraging.

She sang in her family bluegrass band with her father and brother who played guitar. Her father always encouraged her to keep singing and performing, and was always rolling the camera sometimes four or five times a day. Rachel felt comfortable on stage when so many others tightened up. She was nervous sure, but she loved being someone else, emerging in a different person's skin, being able to think a different way, and pretend to be someone else even for a moment.

She performed all throughout high school and decided to major in theatre at a school in Manhattan. She knew it was a long shot to make a career in acting. There were countless waitresses, bartenders, and coffee shop workers who were waiting five, ten, even fifteen years for their big break, and refused to face the reality that it might never come. They clung to their dream by continuing to go to audition after audition only to get rejection after rejection. Rachel was well aware of all that, but she was also aware of how the stage made her feel. That feeling she couldn't escape in a different career. She was a performer at heart and a performer forever.

She had several boyfriends throughout her life. Boys that sweet talked her and said the right words at the right time. Boys that played guitar, rode skateboards, had six packs, tattoos, and smoked pot. Boys that told her they wanted something serious and only wanted it with her, but when they dropped her off at home they told another girl the same exact thing. All of those relationships ended in heartbreaks and mistrust until she met James.

She wasn't ready for something serious when she met James that one night. They had gone to the same high school, but never spoke to each other. He was kind of cute, but not her usual type. No tattoos, no guitar, no bulging muscles, or slick long hair. No smooth one liners, or cocky, borderline arrogant smiles. He was cute when he came up to her and asked her to go out sometime. He stuttered over his words and she could tell he was beyond nervous.

She smiled when she gave him her number. She didn't think he would call or text. He didn't seem like the type that had the courage to do so, and she wasn't ready for anything too serious anyway, but sure enough, he asked her on a date three days later. She was a bit rattled and told him she was busy with her family. He asked again a day or two later, and she said she had plans with her friends. When he asked a third time, she really had to rack her brain for an excuse. She ended up just telling him she was tired and was going to stay in.

James responded with maybe the most important message of her life. He told her that he wanted to get to know her, but that he wasn't going to waste his time. If she wanted to go out great, but if not, they would have to go their own ways. The bluntness of that text, and to call her out like that was attractive. It showcased a side to him that she wanted to know more about.

"Pick me up at 8," she responded, and she quickly got dressed in a yellow tank top and short blue jeans.

It wasn't really a date. Well, maybe it was. She was nervous at first, but he had a calmness about him. He made her feel relaxed with stupid jokes that walked a tightrope of corny and funny. They grabbed ice cream and talked about themselves. She told him about acting and performing and how important her family was to her. He talked about loving to write short stories and poems.

"I'd love to hear them some time," she said smiling as she looked at his blue eyes and shaggy blonde hair.

"They are not good," he responded.

They got back to her house and he walked her to the front door. He told her he had a great time, and she nodded and agreed.

He leaned in for a kiss and her heart stopped. She didn't know if she was ready for that yet. She had to act fast. Quickly she tilted her head to the side as she felt his hand lightly brace her back. Their lips met in perfect contact; soft, supple, secure. She tightened up at first. Her hands almost in fists at her sides, but slowly they released as her fingers straightened, and her hands securely wrapped around his waist.

"Goodnight," she said. "I had a great time."

He nodded. "Me too. Let's do this again."

She smiled and nodded. "You're stuck with me now. You better watch out."

He smiled and slowly walked back to his car. Rachel closed the front door, and then put her back against it, using it to brace herself up. She put her hand over her chest trying desperately to catch her breath with a smile beaming on her face and a tingle all over her body.

They dated for two months at separate colleges. Rachel came home on the weekends and they would go out to dinner or the movies or go out for drinks. Her favorite was just to lie next to him. He held her close in his arms and she felt so special. It sounds silly, but it was like she was the only girl in the world. She brought his hands tightly around her, and when he tried to pull them back to stretch them out, she quickly brought them back to the original position. It was a joke at first, but truly she didn't want him to let go.

Rachel had plans to study abroad. She was going to stay in London, but visit France, Germany, Spain, Greece, and other countries all over Europe. It was a once in a lifetime experience, but she didn't want to lose James. Maybe she shouldn't go. Maybe she needed to stay here and be close to him.

"You need to go," he said. "Don't worry about me. I will be here, and we can talk all the time. Please go. Have fun."

She was reluctant, but she did go. They talked frequently over Skype and FaceTime. She told him about the beaches of Greece, the London Eye, the Holocaust Museum in Germany, the food in France. She missed him though. She couldn't escape this feeling that he wasn't with her to hold her close and tell her that he loved her. She missed the baby blue eyes that looked at her with such a desire. It made her feel like nothing else in this world mattered.

One night, James opened up about his mom. He told her everything. How she had colon cancer and died when he was in middle school. He told her about how he was there in the room as she slowly lost consciousness and the heart machines stopped beeping. She rubbed his back and stroked his hair. She told him how she admired his strength; how his mom would be proud of the man he had become. She told him she loved him, and she meant that with every ounce of her being.

They got married three years later. Rachel performed Tennessee Whiskey for James and the entire wedding venue. She sang each verse with all of her strength. Stretching out her vocal cords with all the power they could muster.

"This is for you and your mom, who can't be here today. I love you, James."

He wiped a tear or two from his eyes as she sang staring at the man of her dreams now in her life forever.

They bought a house a year after that in the same hometown they grew up in Connecticut. A suburban town that was perfect to raise a family with a good school system and a safe neighborhood. Everything was perfect. Everything was exactly how she planned it.

A year later is when everything seemed to change. She went to the bathroom on the thermometer sized stick and looked down to see that one word: *Pregnant.*

She froze. Thinking about what to do. This was it. This was what she had always wanted and it was here. She was going to be a mom. James was at the gym, but she couldn't wait. She texted him. She needed him to come home right away. She took her phone and hid it in a corner and made sure it was recording the video. She took deep breath after deep breath, as she saw his car pull in the driveway, and he opened the front door. She then pulled out the stick from behind her back and showed him the big words that would change their lives forever. He held her close as she lost control. She cried into his shoulder with everything she had. He held her securely around the waist tightly and rocked her side to side.

At first, she was purely excited. She thought about ways to tell their friends and family. She began looking at cribs, bassinets, baby clothes, nursery themes, what diapers to buy, and everything else baby related. She thought about what their baby would look like; a pudgy little kid running around with her green eyes and James 'blonde hair. She smiled when she closed her eyes and tried to picture their future child.

One night she woke up abruptly for some reason. It was not uncommon for her to toss and turn because it was so hard to sleep comfortably pregnant. She looked in the bed and James was not there. She went downstairs and found him passed out on the floor. Luckily, she was able to nudge him awake, and get him up and get to bed.

She was beyond pissed off. How could he get that wasted? How irresponsible and inconsiderate could he be to do that to his pregnant wife at home? She grinded her teeth and shook her head from side to side. She wanted to slap him so hard so that he could hurt like she was hurting, but she didn't. She lied back in bed and closed her eyes hard in an attempt to get sleep.

Slowly, but surely that dark feeling was reappearing. It seemed to grow with every passing day. It clenched to her shoulders and glued to her feet. It tackled her in bed, making it difficult to get up in the morning, and shook her at night, making it nearly impossible to sleep.

She needed a change. She couldn't keep going like this. So one night, she told James she wanted to sleep in the basement and be alone. She could tell that bothered him. He looked shocked and disappointed, but she thought this would help. She just wanted to be alone and try to get some sleep. She gave him the best kiss she could muster. She closed her eyes and puckered her lips. She gave him a light hug and told him she loved him. Then she went down the stairs to the basement to try and sleep.

As she lied on the downstairs couch she thought about the stage. She thought about a sold out crowd of hundreds watching her movements, listening to her voice with undeniable attention. She thought about the sand on her toes on the beaches of Greece. The crystal-clear blue water splashing up to her ankles. She thought about the light in James 'blue eyes that only saw her. That feeling that numbed her whole body; that feeling that overwhelmed her every time he looked at her-- she rubbed her stomach which was protruding out like a small watermelon now. She caressed it in smooth, slow, circular motions, as her back tensed up, her shoulders cramped, and her legs felt weightless. She closed her eyes trying to picture something--anything, but there was nothing to comfort her. All around her was darkness as she kept her hand securely on her stomach and tried to fall asleep all alone.

Chapter 28
Practice Makes Perfect

Coach thought about what to tell his team for the entire weekend. He still had to check himself about how much time he thought about this team. Part of him was thinking dude this is just a middle school football team, don't worry so much, then after a minute, he thought about Lito, Terrell, Vinny, and what they were doing right now. He thought about new plays and formations, ways to get them the ball in space, ways to block better, different drills to try. They played in his head on repeat and cycled over and over again.

Monday's practice was very important. They had five days to prepare for Barrett and hope to dethrone the three-time champions. Overall, practice was very good, they showed good focus, intensity, and effort. Coach reviewed their basic plays; their tosses, dives, and simple throws. Coach knew the most important thing was getting the team to be on the same page mentally. Coach ended practice a little earlier than normal to talk to the guys.

"Gentlemen, when we started this thing no one would have thought we would be here. Our backs were against the wall. Teams were blowing us out, but we came together and we fought and now we are one win away from taking it all."

Coach paused, partly for dramatic effect, but the other part was to think about how he would transition to his next point.

" The most important thing, beyond all else, is that we stay together. We cannot let anything break us apart and take us off our game--"

"But, they were cheating," 'Lito said.

"Facts," Responded Terrell.

Coach nodded. "Yes, they were cheating. I know that, but look at what good it did them? You can't just grab guys off the street, plug them in, and make it work. A good team needs to be a family. We need to fight to become better through good and bad, and we've done that."

He saw some nods and some blank stares.

"The biggest thing we need to do is learn from our mistakes. Things are not going to go our way. People are going to try and get in your head, get under your skin. Don't let them."

"But Coach, if someone comes at us what we supposed to do? I am not taking that from anyone?"

In a way Lito was right. You don't just take it, but how did he say that?

"Yes, but think about this. That dude that smacked you was one of their worst players. He hit you, you hit him back, and you both got kicked out. They got what they wanted. You gave them what they wanted."

Lito shrugged.

"And I'm not coming at you Lito. It can happen to anyone at any time, but we need to be smarter and have self-control."

"So what are we supposed to do? Just let them snuff us?"

Coach took a deep breath.

"Listen, my advice, would be to walk away. Be the stronger person and let your talking be with your pads." It was corny, but it was the best Coach could come up with and he meant it too.

Lito shook his head side to side with cocked smile on his face.

"Coach, you can't walk away. Not here."

Coach looked at Lito and was silent. They exchanged a look of agreement as Coach nodded reluctantly.

"Good practice today boys. Let's keep it up and get ready for the ship this weekend."

They broke down practice as Coach waited for all the kids to get changed and walk down the boulevard. Then Coach got in his car and drove past the boulevard, onto the highway with New Haven barely visible in the rearview mirror as he headed home.

Chapter 29
The Big Game

Coach didn't really know how to take the championship game. Usually, the crowd for their games were minimal, consisting of maybe 20-30 people who were mostly family members. There was no scoreboard, and the field had lines that were barely visible, dirt that outnumbered the grass in many areas, and for unknown reasons, hills and dips instead of a flat surface they were used to.

The championship was a whole different animal and the players and coaches could tell right away. Yes, it was middle school, but it felt bigger than that.

First key difference was it was a night game. All of their games were during the day. 10, 12, or 2. This game was at 6:00. It was played at the high school turf field, which had large bleachers, a huge lit up scoreboard, and speakers that blasted music. There was also a PA announcer who blared "Welcome the Cougars to the field!"

That took even the Coach by surprise. Then he looked at the stands and saw it filled almost entirely with fans. Surprising didn't properly explain how he felt about seeing all those people. It brought a different energy to the game that they had not really seen before. Coach thought about addressing it though because he had a feeling if the boys were too hyped up it could lead to mistakes and problems.

"This is just like any other game we've played," he had to almost shout to talk over the music.

"We've beaten these dudes before, and we can do it again. Just do our jobs and we will be fine."

Many of the players nodded as they began to warm up and go over a couple of their plays. Coach took a deep breath and looked at the stands remembering that it is just a game, it is just middle school, but wondering why he had chills and a deep nervous feeling in his stomach.

***

2 weeks later

Rachel wanted to take a walk that Saturday evening. She liked walks and the doctor said it was good for her to move her legs. It was kind of cold out, especially with the wind kicking in, so Coach and her went to the mall. He hated the mall for a variety of reasons. Shopping bored him to tears, and there were so many people that creeped him out. Plus there were vendors that were always asking to participate in surveys or get you to try something. It was a pain.

"Let's get some pretzel bites. I am starving."

They stopped at the pretzel stand and Coach got her a medium sized cup of pretzel bites and cheese dipping sauce. They walked around the mall some more eating their snack when Rachel stopped for a second.

"You okay?"

"Yeah, just had to stop for a second, I got a cramp in my stomach."

They had gone to the doctor a bunch of times and Coach knew this could be a sign. He thought about movies when the mom's water breaks and the husband and wife hurry into the car and race to the hospital as the baby is popping its way out. The doctor told them that many moms think they are in labor when they really aren't. A lot of times they have to be sent home because they are just not far enough along.

Coach knew that if these were contractions they had to be every minute or so and last about 30 seconds to a minute.

"Okay, well, do you want to stop? Go home?"

"No, I'm fine," Rachel said and they kept walking.

She walked for almost fifteen minutes without any pain or discomfort until she stopped again. It was an abrupt stop like a car at a red light.

"You okay?"

"Yeah, that one hurt a bit," she said as she grabbed her stomach.

"You want to go?"

Rachel nodded, "yeah let's head home. I need to lie down for a bit."

Rachel had some uncomfortable pains, but still nothing too close together. They ate dinner and went to bed when Rachel woke up with a sharper pain in her stomach.

"James, it is wet, there's water all over the bed."

Coach quickly got out of bed. "Okay, let's call the doctor."

They called and asked Rachel some questions. Coach thought it was a no brainer that this baby was coming, but the nurses weren't as sure I guess. They finally told Rachel to go to the hospital so they could check on her.

They got dressed and took their bag, along with all the other stuff Rachel had prepared. She was good about being prepared and having things together. Quite the opposite of him.

Coach drove at a reasonable speed, but with careful intensity.

"Woah…" Rachel said as she grabbed his hand tightly.

"You okay?"

"Yeah, that one just hurt a bit."

They pulled into the hospital parking lot, grabbed their stuff, and walked to the entrance. The desk people asked a couple questions and then brought them to the room. A nurse came in shortly thereafter and asked Rachel to lie down and remove her pants. She inspected Rachel for a moment. Before almost immediately nodding her head.

"So your mucus plug just came out and you are about 4 cm dilated."

The nurse removed her gloves and threw them in the trash.

"It is a good thing you came in. You are going to have this baby today."

Chapter 30
Kickoff

Before the game started the PA announcer called the names of each player as they ran onto the field and stood at the 35-yard line. The teams stood across from one another with their helmets at their sides as the national anthem played over the speakers. Coach would be lying if he didn't admit he was a bit nervous. When the anthem finished, Coach made his way to the sideline. He looked up and saw Rachel and his dad. They gave a wave and he gave one back, but now it was time to focus on the game. Time to bring a championship home to the high school wrestler who never coached a day in his life before this year.

The game started with Barrett getting the ball first. Coach wondered how they would attack them. He knew they had a good passing game, so he had Terrell drop to safety and kept Vinny at one linebacker spot on the right side and Lito as the backer on the left. That strategy seemed to make sense in theory, but it was vulnerable. Barrett ran the ball right up the middle. It was not registering huge gains, but four, five, six-yard gains on every play. It was boring but effective.

"Coach! Move me inside, they are killing us in the middle!" Lito shouted after a play.

Coach shook his head. He knew they were gaining yards, but he did not want to give them the outside. If they got the edge it could result in a big play, maybe even a touchdown. They had to hang in there.

"No! Stay there. We will get it done. Stay outside."

Sure enough, Lito did not listen. Right after the snap, he rushed right inside where he thought the ball was going. He was wrong. The QB faked the handoff perfectly. He then rolled out to where Lito should have been, but wasn't Lito was trapped in a sea of Barrett players in the middle and the QB was all alone as he practically jogged in the end zone for a touchdown. Untouched. It was 7-0 right away.

"That touchdown is on you!" Coach was angry and put his finger right in Lito's chest.

"I need you to play where I tell you to play. This works. You gotta trust me."

Lito didn't say a word. He had his helmet off and a blank stare.

The Cougars got the ball and needed to respond with a drive of their own. Coach hoped to get it going by getting Lito the ball. The problem was Barrett was expecting that. Before the snap, he could see defenders shifting and motioning all over in a very weird defensive formation. It was hard to understand how they were lining up, but whatever it was it was effective. Lito was also making a critical mistake.

There's an old cliché in football to not do too much or take what the defense gives you. Lito was dancing; juking or spinning and trying to make people miss. That sounds like a good idea, but it only works when it is a one on one situation, not when there are a host of defenders there. Lito had the edge a couple times and if he kept running he would have gotten five, seven, maybe even more, but he slowed down and almost invited defenders. That resulted in minimal gains. The Cougars had no choice. They had to punt.

When Barrett got the ball back they tried the same strategy. The runs up the middle registered a couple nice gains, but the defenders up front fought hard and managed to keep the gains minimal. It was third down when the quarterback faked a handoff and then dropped back. Both Vinny and Lito took the bait and ran thinking it was a run. Even Terrell at safety took one or two steps toward the QB. That was all he needed. The QB threw a wobbling pass high in the air. It was not pretty, but it was high enough to be catchable. Terrell had enough time to run to the spot and try to deflect it or maybe even pick it off. Both the receiver and Terrell jumped trying to make a play on the ball. Terrell had his hand high up in the air and narrowly missed the ball, and with incredible concentration, the Barrett receiver caught the ball with two hands. Terrell fell to the ground and the receiver was able to spin and run the rest of the way for another touchdown. 12-0.

"Coach, let me play safety!" Lito said after he returned to the sideline. Coach shook his head.

"No, Terrell was right there. He made a heck of a play. Nothing you can do about it."

Lito shook his head. Coach gave Terrell a pat on the helmet.

"Nothing you could do about that. Great effort, he just made a hell of a play."

Terrell nodded.

The problem with Barrett's strategy was it took up a lot of time. The small runs ran the clock down and kept their offense off the field. There were only five minutes left to get a drive together to try and score in the first half.

Coach tried to go back to Lito pleading with him to just take the yards you get. Lito did not listen. He tried to dance around defenders and make the miss in the backfield. It was third down when Coach called a play-action pass. Terrell faked the handoff to Lito rolled out and hit Vinny for a nice 20-yard gain. Coach then called a fake toss to Lito and a QB keep to the other side. Terrell was able to make a man miss and run to the outside for a 10-yard gain. He then called a fake handoff to Lito and a toss to Vinny to the other side. It worked for a nice 15-yard gain before Vinny was tackled. They were moving quickly and gaining yards, but not quick enough. The first half expired as Terrell ran to the right side as hard as he could, but there were too many Barrett defenders there. He was stopped two yards shy of the goal line as the half expired. They were down 12-0 and would need a comeback to win.

***

Coach could only watch his wife struggle in pain. She was shaking in her bed side to side and gripping the sheets with intensity. They had tubes all in her arms and one device in her crotch that measured the baby's heartbeat.

"You doing okay Rachel?" he asked. It was a stupid question, but he did not know what to ask.

"These really hurt James." he nodded, which was also stupid because he had no idea how much they actually hurt, but he thought that was what he was supposed to do.

"You are doing great I am proud of you."

"How are you doing?" the nurse asked as she entered the room.

"These really hurt. Is there anything you can do?"

The nurse looked at the machines and then back at Rachel.

"I'm sorry honey, but not quite yet. We need to wait a little longer until we can give you the epidural"

Rachel took a deep breath and let out a powerful scream.

"I am really sorry, just try to breathe like you are doing and we will give you the epidural as soon as we can.."

Rachel nodded. The nurse was about to leave when she looked at the screen with some sort of concern.

"Okay, I am just going to have you sit up a bit for me."

They were both concerned, but he helped her get up a bit higher on the couch.

"Okay, and I am going to have you rotate so your back is to me."

The nurse was speaking in a calm voice, but they were both starting to get nervous.

"Why are we doing this? Is everything okay?" Rachel finally asked.

"I am not seeing the baby's heartbeat," the nurse finally said as she rotated her on her knees and began fiddling with devices frantically.

Chapter 31
Second Half

Coach's speech at halftime was to the point and specific. He was not too into the motivational stuff and maybe that was a weakness of his.

"Gentlemen, we are down, but we are not out."

He looked around and was happy to see the boys had fire in their eyes. None seemed to hang their heads. They were focused on Coach and what he was going to say.

"We need to take what they are giving us defensively."

He was talking about Lito but didn't want to call him out specifically.

"Not every play can be a touchdown. Take what they give you, chip away and we will be fine."

"Defensively we just need to stay the course. Stay focused and just make the plays that are there to be made."

He saw some nods from his team.

"They are going to gain yards and that's okay." He paused seeing more reassuring nods, which motivated him to keep going.

"They are not going to score again though. That I promise you."

More nods and even some "yeah's," he could hear from the team.

"We are going to find out a lot about ourselves in this second half. Are we the team that is going to fight back and take this game or are we going to lie down and let them take this from us?"

"We got this Coach." said Lito as he rose to his feet.

"Let's get it boys!" replied Terrell.

Vinny nodded and pumped his fist in the air as they gathered in a huddle.

"Family on three, "1...2..3... Family!" They broke the huddle and jogged to their sideline.

***

"

It is going to be okay Rachel," he said as he held her hand. She was on all fours with her butt sticking out as the nurse was fiddling with the tubes trying to find the right spot.

"I'm scared."

Coach nodded. "I know, but it is going to be okay. Just try to take deep breaths. I am here for you. We are going to get through this. I promise."

She nodded as the nurse continued to fiddle with the device, but there was still no noise and no heartbeat.

***

The Cougars got the ball to start the second half. Coach had a simple plan to get the ball moving and score. He pulled Lito, Vinny, Terrell and Freddy to explain.

"We are going to spread it around. If we give everyone a taste they aren't going to be able to key in on one player."

They nodded agreeing with the plan.

The drive started with a toss to Vinny on the outside with a modest gain of five yards. The next play was a toss the opposite side to Lito for a slightly better ten-yard gain. That followed by Terrell faking a toss keeping the ball and rolling out to the right side for a gain of eight. They were moving, slowly, but surely. They mixed in a couple runs but did not pass on purpose. Coach was saving a pass to try and catch Barrett off guard. Then it was third down and short on the Barrett fifteen-yard line. Coach dialed up a play-action pass. Vinny would run a post. Lito ran a fly and then Freddy would run a slant. When Coach sent in the play he gave Terrell a simple message.

"Don't sleep on Freddy. He will probably wide open on this one."

Terrell took the snap and took three steps. The defense all seemed to close in expecting a run, which was what Coach hoped for, but the problem was Terrell didn't have a ton of time to react. He had to make a quick decision and just hope it was the right one. Vinny and Lito were covered pretty tightly and the throw would be a tough one into tight coverage. Freddy, like Coach had hoped was wide open. Terrell looked at Lito, Vinny, and then had just enough time to see Freddy. The problem was he didn't throw it to him.

Instead, he ducked the would-be defender. Somehow he managed to shake the defender and get free. Another defender came up from the safety spot, but Freddy came out of nowhere and delivered a great block that got just enough of the defender to get free. Terrell was at the ten-yard line and luckily Vinny and Lito saw Terrell running toward the end zone and they turned and started blocking. If they waited a second longer there was a good chance the Barrett defenders would close in and stop Terrell, but that didn't happen. Instead, Terrell had the open field and he was able to get into the end zone for their first touchdown.

The sideline erupted and the crowd erupted as the PA announcer blared "It is a Cougar Touchdown!"

The team exchanged high fives and were jumping up and down in celebration. The score was now 12-7. They needed a touchdown to win but now they needed to play defense and stop Barrett from scoring or it would all be over.

***

It was probably only five minutes of Rachel on her knees in what most have been an uncomfortable position. All Coach could do was hold her hand and try to be positive as the nurse continued to frantically twirl the device between Rachel's legs.

Finally, there was beeping. The monitor they were looking at began to pulsate a bit. They both froze and looked at each other.

"Okay, we are good, that is the heartbeat and it is normal."

They both took deep breaths. Coach helped Rachel lie back down and get more comfortable, maybe not comfortable, but slightly better than the position she was in.

"You did so good babe," Coach said slightly stroking her hair.

Rachel looked like she had just gone through a war. Her eyes were heavy, she was breathing in and out heavily.

"Thank you." was all she managed to say as the beeping of the heartbeat continued. It was music to their ears.

***

Time was running out and they needed to stop Barrett from scoring. If they scored again it would all be over. There were only five minutes left and not enough time to score two touchdowns. Barrett was continuing to move the ball slowly, but surely. Four-yard runs, five-yard runs, ten yards pass, quarterback keep for three more yards. It was frustrating, death by a thousand paper-cuts, but they could not panic. The Barrett coach wanted him to blitz heavily and then he would throw a one on one pass like he did before and the game would be over. Barrett had the ball on the Cougar five-yard line. Luckily the Barrett quarterback fumbled the ball right at snap. The quarterback did the right thing and landed right on the ball keeping the possession, but now it was fourth down. Barrett could throw it or run it. They were effective at both, so Coach was unsure of what they should do. Does he play back in zone or does he get aggressive and send a blitz? He decided to take a chance and call an all-out blitz. He gave the signal to Lito, Terrell, and Vinny to all blitz right on the snap. If they got there the play had no chance no matter what it was, but if they didn't it, meant a touchdown and the end of the game, and the end of their season. It was a gamble, but one he was willing to go for.

The Barrett quarterback took the snap and all three of them reacted at the perfect time. Vinny and Lito broke through the line and were right in the quarterback's face with Terrell not too far behind. The quarterback had no choice but to throw the ball out of bounds. Turnover on downs. It would now be Cougars' ball with a chance to score a touchdown and win the game. But they had a long way to go and not a lot of time.

***

Things kind of settled down a bit after they found the baby's heartbeat. Normally you see movies and tv shows where the couples rush to the hospital and the baby pops right out after a couple pushes. That was what Coach was expecting, but that was not the case. What really happened were a series of pushes by Rachel every couple minutes. The baby would come out little by little, until it was time for delivery. The process could take several hours. Luckily Rachel was feeling better and the pushing was slightly uncomfortable, but not overwhelming. Well, I guess that is easy for the Coach to say. He was obviously not the one pushing.

Several hours passed of pushing, but still no baby. The nurse said everything was fine, but Coach could tell there was a slight nervous look on her face as she looked at the monitors and then checked on the baby. Rachel must have noticed that look too.

"Is everything okay?"

The nurse didn't respond right away, as if she was trying to find the right words, which added to the anxiety.

"The baby is fine she is just a little late to the party. It is not dangerous, but she may need some help on getting out."

Rachel and Coach nodded at each other. They exchanged uneasy looks, but they didn't say anything.

"I'm just going to grab the doctor really quickly."

The nurse left the room and returned minutes later with the doctor.

"So, we are thinking about using something to help the baby get out."

Rachel nodded.

"Right now she is getting stuck on your pelvic bone and we are unable to position her in the right spot so she can get out safely."

She paused for a moment to see if they were going to say anything.

"We are thinking the best action is to use a suction device to help position the baby correctly and get her out safely and easily. It will not harm the baby and it is the safest and easiest way for us to get your baby out."

Rachel and Coach looked at each other.

"What do you think?" she asked.

"I think if the doctors think it is the best plan we should probably go for it. What do you think?"

Rachel took a second and then nodded.

"I agree let's do it."

The doctor and nurse nodded as they left and got ready.

***

There were only three minutes left now with one timeout. They had to go 90 yards and they had to score a touchdown. Coach knew there was still time, but they had to work quickly.

"We don't have lots of time. We need to get on the ball and snap it quickly."

Coach stuck with the plan of spreading the ball around that worked before. The problem was it took time to get the plays in to Terrell, and time was not something they had a lot of. The first play was a pass. Terrell threw a perfect pass to Vinny that he caught and ran toward the twenty-five-yard line. Terrell then tossed it to Lito who managed to get to the outside and get to the forty-yard line for a twenty-yard gain. Coach called another pass, but it seemed like everyone was covered, so Terrell ran passed the fifty before he was pushed out of bounds.

Just under two minutes left and Coach called another pass. Lito was covered, but Terrell threw it to him anyway. The ball hung in the air and Lito did a great job of timing his jump perfectly. He simply out jumped the Barrett defender and snagged the ball as the defender pulled him to the ground at the thirty-yard line. One minute left.

Coach called a toss to Vinny and told him to get out of bounds. Vinny took the toss and ran hard to the edge, Vinny was able to get to the twenty-yard line, but the defenders were smart and kept him in bounds. There was only thirty-five seconds left. They took a timeout.

***

For most of the delivery process it was just Coach, Rachel, and the nurse. In a way, it was a calm process. Rachel pushed as Coach and the nurse held her legs up in the air. Then they would stop, the nurse would check the monitor, and then Rachel would push again. This process would continue for hours.

Now things were very different. Four female doctors entered the room covered head to toe in gloves, aprons, and heavy-duty masks. They got into position quickly as the doctors set up the tools on the table right by her. Coach remained by her side holding her hand telling her it was going to be okay.

"Okay, we are going to get started in a moment. We need to work quickly to get this baby out safely. You okay?" The doctor's voice was muffled because of the mask, but they heard her clearly.

They both nodded as Rachel held his hand the tightest he had ever felt.

***

"Family!" the team all said as they broke the huddle. This was their season and their chance to win it all. Coach grabbed Terrell before he went onto the field.

"Freddy is going to be open on this play."

Terrell nodded.

"If it is there, give him the chance. It may be the best option."

Terrell nodded again.

Terrell got under center and took the snap. The defense was expecting a pass because they dropped into coverage. Terrell looked to his right at Lito and he was totally covered. He then turned to the left and looked at Vinny who was also surrounded by defenders. There were defenders starting to close in on Terrell. One from his right and one from his left. There were two starting to fight off blocks in front of him and get in his face.

Finally, Terrell glanced at Freddy who was wide open. Terrell hesitated, pumping the football, as if it was his last resort to throw it to Freddy, he didn't seem to trust Freddy's hands, which was not all that unfair, but he threw it anyway. He managed to get the ball out as defenders closed in on him. Terrell hit the ground with a powerful thud as the ball rotated in Freddy's direction.

The ball lofted in the air in a very catchable way, but Freddy didn't seem to expect it and he bobbled it as it hit his hands. It then popped in the air high above his head. That was a dangerous situation as any football player or Coach will tell you, but somehow Freddy kept the ball in his sights as it hit his hands again and popped in the air a second time until it finally landed almost perfectly in his grasp.

Freddy had to slow down to catch the ball, which gave Barrett defenders some time to close in. There were three defenders closing in on Freddy, two from behind and one from the end zone. Freddy ran as fast as he could. He made it to the ten, then the five, as defenders started to close in, it was going to be a photo finish. Freddy met the defender right at the goal line, lowering his shoulder trying to muscle his way into the end zone as the defenders grabbed Freddy from behind and tried to pull him backward. Vinny came in from what seemed out of nowhere and tried to pull Freddy to the end zone. Lito came from the other side and did the same thing. Freddy inched closer and closer to the goal line every millisecond. Then Terrell came as fast as he could and lowered his shoulder and gave a huge shove trying to get Freddy past the goal line. Freddy gritted his teeth, held onto the ball with all his might as he tried to get across the goal line.

The whistle blew emphatically as Freddy hit the ground. Bodies were all around Freddy and it was hard to tell where he was amongst the pile of players. The refs rushed in to pull off all the players to sort out where Freddy had landed. Player after player began to come off the pile and rise to their feet. Both Barrett players and Cougar players one by one rose and looked at the scene like detectives sorting out a crime scene. Then it was just Freddy with the ball in his hands, sprawled out as far as he could stretch with the ball securely in his right hand. Barrett players began jumping up and down with their hands in the air. Freddy was mere inches short of the goal line.

Chapter 32
Honor and Light

The doctors were covered head to toe in what looked more like hazmat suits instead of scrubs. Coach felt like it was more appropriate for Chernobyl instead of the delivery room of a hospital, but he tried to remain calm for his wife and his future daughter.

"James, I am scared." Rachel said as she squeezed his hand tightly.

He nodded and squeezed back.

"I know, but you are doing great. I am going to be right here. I promise." He pushed her hair back and gently kissed her on the top of her forehead.

"You are doing great. I am so proud of you."

The doctors were setting up tools carefully near Rachel's legs at the end of the hospital bed.

"Rachel, this is very common. We are going to use this suction to help the baby come out safely."

She held up what looked like a plunger on top with a small handle along with a pump you would use for a basketball.

"It will not harm the baby at all. She just might have a little mark on her like when you suck on a bottlecap, but that will go away within a day or two."

They both nodded. The major thing was getting their daughter out safely and they trusted the doctors to do that even though this experience was a little intimidating.

The doctors quickly got in position. Three were by the bottom part of Rachel, while one was checking the machine and the nurse stood by Rachel's left.

"I'm going to ask you to push Rachel."

She took a deep breath and gave it all she had. Grunting and teeth clenched. She even let out a "Ugh!" which indicated how hard she was pushing.

"That's great Rachel. Just like that. I need a couple more of those."

Coach looked down and could see a small ball appearing in between Rachel's legs. It didn't look anything like a human.

"Push Rachel. Come on you can do it."

Another aggressive push from Rachel and that ball moved further out. Coach could see what looked like hair. Greasy jet-black hair on top of this ball shape.

"Excellent, we are almost there! One more big one!"

Rachel geared up and gave another big "Ugh!" as she clenched her fists and gripped the bedsheets tightly.

Coach looked down and saw a head. It was not completely round. It was a unique oval like shape, but it looked like a head for sure.

"Here she comes!"

Then almost instantly the doctor pulled the head carefully, yet forcefully. There were a pair of legs and arms, which were in perfect proportion to this red little body. The doctor turned it around slowly and there she was. Coach saw his daughter for the first time. Her eyes swollen shut as if she got into a boxing fight. Her little hands clenched into fists and then relaxing. Her toes kicking slightly in this newfound environment.

The doctor put her on Rachel's chest. Coach quickly swelled up in tears as he rubbed her small little back and felt her sticky hair. She was the most beautiful thing he had ever seen.

"Congratulations, you guys! She is beautiful."

***

After the game, there was a ceremony for the winning team. Coach kind of hoped they could just go to the sideline, talk quickly and then go home, but instead they had to kneel at the fifty-yard line and watch Barrett celebrate their third straight title.

The athletic director Ralph came over and shook his hand.

"Great job this year. Seriously, thank you for all you did for the kids and the program. "

He nodded and appreciated the kind words.

"No problem. It was fun and a pleasure."

Ralph then walked in between the teams with the microphone.

"What a great game and a great season."

Ralph pointed at Cougars and then motioned to Barrett.

"But we have to congratulate our back, to back, to back champions... the Barrett Falcons!"

The crowd erupted and all the coaches from the Barrett side dumped a giant bucket of Gatorade on the head coach. Coach V had secretly hoped that would have been him. He hoped he would be the one engulfed in Gatorade and smiling ear to ear, but he was on the other side. His hands in his pockets watching.

The Barrett coach took the trophy and held it up high in the air. The Barrett players came rushing over in a mosh pit of celebration. They were jumping up and down each one trying to touch the trophy.

"Come on guys, let's get over to our sideline. I want to say a couple things."

They took a slow walk to the sideline with their helmets in their hands. They took a knee right on the sideline away from the Barrett celebration.

"Listen, I want to thank you guys for an incredible season. You guys fought hard and have absolutely nothing to be ashamed of."

He paused and wiped his mouth. He could see several players looking over at Barrett continue their celebration. Some were crying visibly, but some stared right at him. Vinny looked right into his eyes so directly it almost pierced him.

"Be proud of what you did this year, how far we came and how hard you fought.."

Coach V could feel a presence behind him. He spun around and saw Coach Bryant.

"Sorry to interrupt Coach, but I wanted to say great job."

They exchanged handshakes and a half hug.

"Thanks coach. I appreciate that."

"You mind if I say a couple words to the boys when you are done?"

Coach V nodded. "Please, go right ahead."

Coach Bryant stepped up. He was a massive human being. He folded his big arms covered with tattoos across his chest.

"Gentlemen, I want to say congrats on a great season. You got here, which is an incredible accomplishment."

He paused as he slightly stroked his chin.

"I know this feeling sucks and I want you to think about how you feel right now and never get used to it. Never accept it, and do what you can to get past it."

Coach V was nodding emphatically behind him.

"All you can do is give it your all. If you truly gave all you had, ran your fastest, blocked your hardest, tackled your hardest. If you really gave max effort, then you can do no more."

Coach Bryant stuck out his finger

"But I repeat, never get used to this feeling. Never, ever, get used to it."

Coach scanned the team. He looked at Vinny, Terrell, Lito, and Freddy. There was a small light glistening in their eyes as some of them nodded their heads while others just stared intently. The light was so small, barely a sliver, maybe it was a mirage, maybe his mind was playing tricks on him, or maybe what Coach Bryant said was true. Or maybe that was just what he wanted to believe.

***

The doctors quickly took the baby and performed some tests. She weighed seven pounds and five ounces. She was 21 inches long and her head circumference was 13 inches.

"She's perfect." the doctor said as she handed her to Coach V.

"Do you guys have a name yet? I need to put it on her chart."

Coach nodded. "Nora."

"Very, pretty. I love that name."

He nodded again as he rocked her back and forth. He was shocked that she was not crying as her eyes were closed shut and her mouth slightly perked open.

Rachel and Coach V had talked about names for a while, and they both settled on Nora after hearing the way it sounded. Short, simple, and it felt right, then they discovered the name meant honor and light and that sounded perfect; two things they hoped to instill in her; to always be your true self, and to always shine bright, no matter the challenge or predicament, even when things seemed hopeless or desperate.

He continued to rock Nora back and forth slowly side to side. He thought about the Cougars: Vinny, Terrell, Lito, and Freddy lying almost as hopelessly on the field just as Nora was now. They fought as hard as they could, gave everything they had, but it wasn't enough.

He thought about his mom fighting to keep her eyes open in a hospital room that was eerily similar to the one they were in now. He squeezed her hand with careful strength just as he squeezed Nora's small body close to his chest.

Then he looked at Rachel, her battle of over 14 hours in labor finally over, and the fruits of her efforts lay carefully in his arms. He loved her with all his heart and he always would, but he wondered if that would be enough.

Amidst the rocking, Nora opened her eyes ever so slightly. They were big pools of black that slowly looked up and made contact with him. Nora's little hand clenched his chest as those little black pools glistened and he rocked her gently tucked away in his arms.

Author James Voytek is a middle school language arts teacher in New Haven Connecticut. He has also been a coach of football and basketball for over four years at the middle school level. James received a BA in English from Southern Connecticut State University and an MBA in Education from Post University. He currently lives in Trumbull Connecticut with his wife Sarah and his daughter Nora.

CPSIA information can be obtained
at www.ICGtesting.com
Printed in the USA
BVHW04021518 0920
589100BV00015B/658

9 781952 894398